Rats, Mice, And Dormice As Pets

The Complete Owner's Guide

Care, health, keeping, raising, training, food, costs, where to buy, breeding, and much more all included!

By: Lolly Brown

Foreword

I have two specific personal memories involving rodents. One of these stories also involves my mother. The two should never be mixed.

When I was in college, a poor, unsuspecting little mouse wandered into my mother's bathroom and into a box of tissues. Mother reached for one and came up with a very terrified little creature instead.

She screamed, the mouse ran for its life, and Mother promptly slammed the bathroom door, wedged a bath towel under the threshold, and summoned my father to come home from his business.

Dutiful man that he was, he drove home only to ask the most obvious question of all, "We have six cats. Why did you call me?"

The largest of my cats was retrieved and set loose in the bathroom, but no sign of the mouse was ever seen again. Daddy always said the poor thing went off and died of a heart attack.

The second incident occurred roughly in the same period when I was taking a summer class in Field Biology. We were tagging local wildlife as part of a conservation project and accidentally caught a large cotton rat.

We set the cage aside, planning to release the animal later. Instead, the class was treated to a 15 minute exercise in rodent intelligence. As we watched, the rat minutely examined every inch of the cage, studying the trap door mechanism and experimentally applying pressure here and there.

Then, he sat down in the middle of the cage, obviously thinking. About five minutes passed. The rat suddenly stood up, walked to the front of the cage, applied his weight to the trap door, shoved it open, and scampered out of the cage.

Our dumbfounded instructor said, "But it's not supposed to open from the inside." Someone forgot to tell the rat.

I'm afraid I have no personal dormouse story to tell you, beyond the fact that I've admired the little creatures in the homes of friends and have been absolutely charmed by their over-sized eyes and winsome personality.

Although companion rodents are not long-lived pets, they are among the smartest creatures I have ever encountered. Contrary to popular belief, they are clean, have no odor when cared for properly, and are highly affectionate.

Many people do not know that the rodent "fancy" encompasses a thriving show culture with intricate breeding programs and pedigrees that rival that of any purebred dog or cat.

Rats, mice, and dormice also have the added advantage of taking up very little space, a decided plus for apartment dwellers, and they are quiet — also a positive as you won't have to be dealing with neighbors complaining about any noise.

In the following pages, I hope to introduce you to the world of companion rodents and to explain the basics of their care, from buying the supplies you will need to create a habitat, to feeding, and health care.

While a rat or a mouse might not be the perfect pet for you, at the very least I hope to leave you with an appreciation for the many fine qualities these little creatures exhibit, and to remove any erroneous perceptions you have of them as destructive vermin.

Fancy rats and mice, and dormice are fully domesticated and utterly charming pets that will make excellent and endearing additions to your home and family life.

Acknowledgements

I would like to express my gratitude towards my family, friends, and colleagues for their kind co-operation and encouragement which helped me in completion of this book.

I would like to express my special gratitude and thanks to my loving husband for his patience, understanding, and support.

My thanks and appreciations also go to my colleagues and people who have willingly helped me out with their abilities.

Additional thanks to my children, whose love and care for our family pets inspired me to write this book.

Table of Contents

Table of Contents

Table of Contents

Table of Contents

Table of Contents

Chapter 1 - Rats, Mice, and Dormice

Approximately 40% of the earth's entire mammal population is comprised of rodents. Antarctica is the only continent where rodents don't live.

It's common knowledge that rats and mice are rodents, but so are squirrels, beavers, and porcupines.

A rodent's teeth are specially adapted to chew dense materials. Rodents not only gnaw their food, they also create their homes and make their bedding by gnawing.

For this reason, rodents' upper and lower incisors grow throughout their lives, and must be kept constantly worn down. When kept as pets, this means a vital part of husbandry is supplying adequate hard toys for gnawing.

What are Rats?

Rats are the most intelligent of all the rodents, although squirrels run them a close second. In the wild, there are two species of rats: *Rattus rattus*, the roof rat, and *Rattus norvegicus*, the Norway rat.

The two species cannot interbreed, but are still closely related. Roof rats arrived in America first, although an exact date is not known. Norway rats, however, were reported in the British colonies by 1775.

Today, roof rats are found on both U.S. coastlines and in the American South. The Norway rat is more widely distributed in America, and is also common in Canada and England.

Roof Rats

Roof rats originated in India and are well adapted to tropical climates. They have long tails, large ears, and a somewhat delicate build. You will also see these animals referred to as tree, ship, and black rats.

Norway Rats

The Norway rat is the larger and more common of the two species. It is often called the brown, wharf, sewer, house, or barn rat. It is the direct ancestor of the domesticated rats kept as pets by enthusiasts.

Norway rats originated in an area of Russia located near the Caspian Sea. They are heavier in build and have small ears. By nature this species is better adapted to cooler climates.

Many of the qualities of the Norway rat have been selectively bred into companion domestic rats. They are highly adaptable creatures and opportunistic in their approach to survival.

Their shopping list of abilities include skills at:

- climbing
- digging
- jumping
- swimming

They have been known to chew through both lead and concrete, and can leap as much as four feet / 1.22 meters. On average, a wild Norway rat weights 10-17 ounces / 284 – 482 grams. The largest ever measured, however, was 23 inches / 58.42 cm long and weighed 2 lbs. 12 oz. / 962 grams.

Domesticated Rats

Domestic rats are very similar in appearance to wild Norway rats. They are, however, extremely docile and receptive to being handled by humans. They are much less aggressive and predatory.

Because domestic rats reach sexual maturity as early as five weeks and produce large litters, they reproduce quickly and easily in the pet trade. They are completely domesticated and would not be able to survive well on their own if turned loose.

Socialization is necessary, however, especially in the critical period of age 2-4 weeks. Rats are highly social with one another and bond with equal strength to their humans, happily grooming, playing, sleeping, and eating with their people.

Because there are so many varieties of domesticated or "fancy" rats, all the various types will be discussed in the next chapter along with fancy mice.

What are Mice?

Mice are physically much smaller than rats. Some people feel this makes them cuter, but that is a matter of personal preference on the part of the owner.

Luxurious whiskers flank a mouse's pointed snout. When a mouse twitches those whiskers curiously, he makes for a most beguiling sight.

Whiskers or "vibrissae" are also found on the upper lips, and a single whisker is located under each bright, inquisitive eye. Shorter whiskers are located on the chin.

These specialized hairs help mice to sense movements in the air as compensation for their limited visual acuity. They do, however, have a keen sense of smell that further augments their navigational skills.

A mouse uses his front feet in a very hand-like fashion to hold his food and to grasp objects. The front feet have four toes, while the back have five. Mice stand well on their hind feet, and will often assume an upright posture when they find something particularly interesting and worthy of investigation.

Common House Mouse

Mus musculus, the common house mouse is the best-known variety. It has an agouti coat, which, at first glance appears brown. Actually, each individual hair sports ticked bands of color. The muzzle and feet are more lightly shaded, and the tails is long and hairless.

Mice use their tails to help them achieve their trademark acrobatic scampering. As they leap and climb, tackling unsteady surfaces with great ease, their tails function as both a counterweight and a "fifth" stabilizing leg.

Feeder Mice

Feeder mice are the most readily available type in the United States where they are sold as live food for reptiles, a practice that is illegal in the United Kingdom. These mice are raised with no regard to their genetic quality, and are usually poorly fed and housed in deplorable conditions.

Feeder mice are cheap, and can be bought for $.30-$.50 / £0.18-£0.30 each. Typically, however, they can only be purchased in large lots unless a store manager can be cajoled into selling one or two as pets.

It is difficult to obtain a healthy feeder mouse, but with love and attention, they can be turned into good companions. Unfortunately, however, feeder mice have a lifespan of one year or less as compared to 2 – 2.5 years for fancy mice.

Fancy Mice

The world of fancy mice, like that of fancy rats, is extensive and convoluted. The following chapter is dedicated exclusively to these elite animals, who are so pampered, many of them have fine and complicated pedigrees! They are, indeed, the royalty of the rodent world and are as highly prized by their owners as any other type of show animal.

Laboratory Mice

Both BALB/c or C57BL/6 lab mice make superb pets if you know someone who can acquire the animals for you. The BALB/c is an albino strain of the common house mouse, while the C57BL/6 is extensively used in human disease testing. They are prolific, reproducing easily, and have extremely robust and hardy constitutions.

Wild Mice

Wild mice do not make good pets. They are wary by nature, and don't usually calm down even when treated with great kindness. Wild mice also carry zoonotic diseases, meaning they can be transferred to humans, a topic that will be covered in detail in the chapter on health.

What Are Dormice?

Dormice are also rodents, and are primarily found in Europe, with some species indigenous to Africa and Asia. They are members of the family *Gliridae*. Only one species is native to Britain, the hazel dormouse, a whimsical little creature that has found its way into many children's stories and illustrations.

Dormice range in size from 2.4 to 7.5 inches (6-19 cm) and weigh 0.53 to 6.35 ounces (15-180 grams). Many species live in trees and are nocturnal. Consequently, they are very well adapted to climbing. Although mouse-like in appearance, a dormouse has a furred tail and often over-sized eyes.

Dormice are omnivores, but subsist largely on a diet of fruits and berries, flowers and nuts, and insects. They produce one to two litters per year averaging four offspring following a gestation period of 22-24 days.

Depending on the region in which they live, a dormouse may hibernate for six months or longer. Their lifespan is roughly four years.

These creatures are relatively new in the pet trade, with the most popular species kept as a companion being the African Pygmy Dormouse. Sometimes called "microsquirrels," the species is small and agile. They are not pets that are good for handling or interactive play, but they are fascinating to watch provided you are a night owl.

In the world of rodents, I would definitely characterize dormice as exotics. They aren't for everyone, and are likely not a "beginners" rodent. Once a dormouse escapes, it's extremely difficult to recapture. This is certainly not a pet a child can handle alone. I am including dormice in this book as a class of "advanced" companion rodent.

History of the Rodent Fancy

The history of rodents living with humans is long and convoluted, beginning with an involuntary relationship on the part of mankind. When we ceased to be primarily hunters and gatherers, shifting to a more agrarian existence, rats and mice happily moved into grain storage bins, helping themselves to our food.

This is, in fact, how cats came to be domesticated as companions to human beings. They earned their keep in the granaries exterminating the rodents, fulfilling their side of the equation in one of the oldest of all adversarial relationships in the animal kingdom.

Not all civilizations, however, viewed rodents as a scourge to be served up to the cats for the taking. In Asia, where mice are believed to have originated, the Chinese kept the tiny animals as pets as early as 1100 BC. The Egyptians accorded supernatural powers to mice, while the Greeks used them in rituals for divination and prophesy.

(Alas, dormice faced a different fate in the same period. The Romans considered them a succulent edible delicacy!)

The first mice and rats to be kept as pets by humans were undoubtedly wild specimens with the typical agouti or brown coloration. Both species, however, quickly adapted to domestication and were easily improved by selective breeding to enhance not only their temperament, but also their size and coat color, quality, and texture.

The mouse fancy can be traced to 18th century Japan with the publication of the booklet, "The Breeding of Curious Varieties of the Mouse." The hobby was present in England by the late 19th century where the National Mouse Club was founded in 1895 thanks to the work of Walter Maxey, the "father" of the hobby.

In 1901 the National Mouse Club agreed to include rats at the request of Miss Mary Douglas, now considered to be the "mother of the rat fancy." In 1912, the organization changed its name to the National Mouse and Rat Club. After her death, however, the interest in rats declined, and the club reverted to its original name in 1929.

In roughly this same period, mice and rats were increasingly used in scientific research, most notably the genetic work of Gregor Mendel. This led to the breeding of more unusual specimens, which in turn stimulated greater interest in "fancy" rats and mice as pets.

In January 1976, the National Fancy Rat Society was founded in Great Britain, and exists today in concert with the original National Mouse Club.

The proliferation of the rodent fancy in the United States does not enjoy the same precise documentation. It's likely that the first companion rodents in the U.S. were either wild mice or laboratory animals. In the 1950s, The American Mouse Club was formed, but was quickly abandoned.

In 1978, the American Fancy Rat and Mouse Association was created, and is still the flagship organization for the hobby in the United States.

Rats, Mice, and Dormice as Pets

Rats make excellent pets. They are very easy to look after, as well as being clean and quiet. The same is true of mice, that are, by nature, gentle, loving, and curious animals.

Although both species are smart, gregarious, and interactive, rats do edge mice out in the intelligence department. Pet rats easily learn their names, pick up extensive vocabularies from their humans, and are receptive to training.

Rats also love to "ride" around on their people, and will quite happily cling to your shoulder as you go about your daily business.

Due to their high level of intelligence, rats do need a lot of time and attention from their humans and will become unhappy and even sick if they don't get it.

Typically rats do live longer, but on average, both rats and mice survive only 2 to 2.5 years. Mice are the more fragile, weighing just 1-2 ounces (28.3-56.69 grams), but next to the African Pygmy Dormouse, they're huge.

An African Pygmy Dormouse has an average body length of 3.54 inches / 9 cm (excluding the tail) and weighs 0.63-1.05 ounces (18-30 grams.)

All of these creatures are nocturnal, but rats are generally willing to adjust to your comings and goings. Mice can be especially given to nighttime escapes until they settle down to their life with you. Dormice? Don't turn your back on those little guys or leave their cage top off for a second!

Never make the mistake of keeping any of your rodent pets in the bedroom with you. Rats are busy by nature, and mice can be absolutely manic — as can dormice. Both of these creatures are either running at top speed, or conked out sound asleep. If your pets are in the room with you and they have a squeaky exercise wheel, sleep for you is not an option.

Rats, mice, and dormice are all fastidious, and there will be no undue odor to the habitat if you do your job and clean up after your pets daily. Both mice and rats will pick one corner of their cage to urinate and defecate, which makes your job of spot cleaning each day much, much easier!

Discussing Life Span

Of the three animals, dormice will live the longest, but I do not recommend them as children's pets. If, however, you are buying a rat or a mouse for a child, having a discussion about lifespan from the beginning is crucial.

It is rare for a mouse to live more than three years, although it is quite possible with rats. How you care for these animals will clearly enhance their longevity. Not allowing your rats or mice to become obese, for instance, is very important in extending their life.

This alone is an excellent reason for parents to be involved in the care of pet rodents. Rats and mice that get a steady diet of treats will not do well. Regardless, however, children must be prepared for the inevitable with this sort of pet.

In truth, it's always best to keep multiple mice and rats. This doesn't negate the impact of the death of an individual pet, but it will ease the period of grief.

Allergies

Neither rats nor mice are hypoallergenic. Rodents can, in fact, cause more allergic reactions in humans than dogs or cats. If your child has known allergies, it's probably better to go with a pet turtle or lizard (bearing in mind that these animals can also carry salmonella.)

Do understand, however, that allergies are specific to species. Typically the reaction is to the proteins found in the sebaceous and salivary glands. A child with an allergy to cats may not react to a dog or to mouse, for that matter.

If you are concerned, have your child tested for the kind of pet you are considering acquiring. Better to be out the price of the test than to have a heartbroken child when the pet has already moved in and then must be re-homed.

With Children

As with any kind of pet, consider your child's maturity level and ability to assume responsibilities before getting a rat or a mouse. Both animals are small and can be injured severely if handled incorrectly, or if dropped.

Rats and mice must be fed correctly, and their cages must be kept clean. Rats, in particular, need daily interaction. Dormice, with their diminutive size and high activity profile, should only be considered as pets for older children who are extremely conscientious and reliable.

In general, it's best not to allow a child under the age of 9 to have sole charge of caring for either rats or mice. Even beyond that age, parents should take at least a supervisory role in the husbandry of the pets.

Children of all ages should be properly educated on being gentle and kind with animals, both physically and verbally. Rats have better vision than mice, but both animals have acute hearing and will be frightened and stressed by sudden loud noises.

With Other Pets

When someone asks me if a pet mouse or rat will get along with the family dog or cat, I am often tempted to ask the person if they understand the concept of "prey."

No matter how "nice" your cat may be, a rodent looks like lunch in his eyes. The same is typically true for dogs, especially terriers who were, as breeds, developed to be "ratters."

The only way to keep a successful multi-species household when you mix rodents, dogs, cats — and ferrets, birds, and snakes, for that matter — is a strict policy of segregation. Your rodents will thank you!

Pros and Cons of Rodents as Pets

All of the following points should be considered before you acquire a pet rodent. Only you can decide if these things are pros or cons.

- Rats and mice have relative short lifespans. Dormice live longer, but are not suitable pets for handling.

- Rats, and mice to a lesser degree, are highly trainable. Rats enjoy being held, and some, as you will see, can even be harness trained, but they are still not as interactive as dogs and cats.

- Mice must be kept in a habitat and not allowed to roam free. Some people do allow their rats to have free access in a room or rooms, but those areas must be stringently rat proofed.

- Rats, mice, and dormice are all nocturnal, so you don't want to keep them in an area where anyone is trying to sleep.

- These are small creatures that can be easily injured if handled incorrectly or dropped.

- All rodents can trigger severe allergic reactions in people.

There are, however, certainly some clear cut advantages to keeping rodents as pets:

- high intelligence
- low expense
- minimal space
- cheap maintenance including food
- no noise
- clean
- little to no odor

With fancy mice and rats, there is also the possibility of pairing your ownership of a pet with the hobby of showing the animal in competitive exhibitions.

Chapter 2 - The World of the Rodent Fancy

Fancy rodents do inhabit a whole "world" of variety, one that can be both confusing and overwhelming. The best way to become conversant with all the wonderful colors, patterns, and combinations is to attend a rat and mouse show.

You will never again think of a mouse as "plain" or a rat as "ordinary" once you've seen just how beautiful these domesticated animals really are!

(Since dormice are not shown in competitive exhibitions, they will not be discussed in this chapter.)

Body Types

There are three body types in mice:

- English
- tailless
- gremlin

Rats have three body types:

- standard
- dumbo
- tailless

The term "English" doesn't really describe a body type, so much as designating a mouse that has English blood. "Tailless" is self-explanatory for both mice and rats. The preference is that there be no tail at all, but if a shortened tail is present, it must be perfectly straight.

Gremlin mice have one normally placed ear, and one on the side of their head. Standard rats have ears that are upright and well-spaced with an oval shape. Dumbo rats have large round ears that form low semi-circles on the side of the head.

Coat Varieties

In fancy mice there are 12 potential coat varieties:

- standard
- satin

- angora
- long hair
- rex
- caracul
- texel
- frizzy
- fuzzy
- hairless
- rhino hairless
- rosette

For rats there are seven coat varieties:

- standard
- rex
- satin
- satin rex
- hairless
- double rex
- dwarf

Coats Common to Rats and Mice

For both rats and mice, the ***standard coat*** is dense and thick, with a glossy, lustrous shine. The coats lie flat, but in male rats, slightly longer and coarser guard hairs are permissible. Whiskers should be long and straight.

In rats and mice with ***satin coats***, the hair is thinner, and very fine to the touch but with an exceptionally glossy sheen. In rats, longer guard hairs may be present, but they should not be coarse, and the whiskers are wavy and point in various directions.

For rats and mice with *rex coats*, the fur lays in waves. In mice, the coat progresses through three stages of development: curly at birth, standing out in all directions, and wavy. In rats, there are obvious guard hairs that can be felt. In both species, the whiskers are curled.

In *hairless* rats and mice, the animals should be as hairless as possible, with any color and markings allowed. Hairless mice have no whiskers, but if whiskers are present on hairless rats, they must be curled. Rhino hairless mice are identical to hairless, but with deep wrinkling of the skin and oversized ears.

Specific Mice Coats

Some coat types specific to show mice include the *angora*, which has longer than normal hair with a wool-like consistency and a distinctive "zig zag" pattern. Variations include the Angora Fuzzy and the Angora Rex.

If no zig zag pattern is present, then the mouse is simply said to be a *long hair*. Again, all combination types are possible, like Long Hair Rex or Long Hair Satin.

Caracul mice have coats with a noticeable wave, but it straightens out more as they age, and so is not as pronounced as that of a rex although it is plush to the touch. The whiskers come in straight, but start to curl after a few days.

Texel mice do have tightly curled fur across the whole body with curly whiskers. The guard hairs are thick, curled, and widely dispersed, remaining in place throughout adulthood.

Frizzy mice are smiler, but the hair is not as curly or crimped in appearance. Overall, however, the texture is coarser and the "frizziness" is quite apparent. *Fuzzy* mice may have little to no hair, or very thick, curly hair, but their whiskers are curled or crimped.

Finally, **rosette** mice have whorls of fur placed on each hip in spirals that oppose the standard direction of the main fur.

Specific Rat Coats

Two of the rat specific coats are actually combinations, the Satin Rex and the Double Rex. The **Satin Rex** fur is densely curled and thick with a coarse, but not harsh texture. The whiskers are short and curl around the muzzle in the direction of the mouth. The satin sheen is pronounced and evident even in the presence of the curling.

The **Double Rex** coat can vary from the appearance of a partially sheared lamb or even a poodle to a "buzz cut." There may be small areas of "peach fuzz" on the muzzle, legs, and at the base of the tail. Both the whiskers and the eyelashes should be curled.

Although technically not a coat type, there is another distinct variation, **Dwarf** rats. They are about one-half to one-third the size of standard rats. Their eyes are big in proportion to the size of their heads, and their ears may also appear overly large. They have busy personalities and are known for exceptionally high levels of energy.

Recognized Mouse Colors

There is an almost dizzying combination of possible colors and patterns in the world of fancy mice. Beginning with the 19 recognized solid or "self" colors. These include:

- **black (non-**agouti**)** - Jet black with dark eyes, juveniles display yellow at the base of the tail, ears, genitals, and nipples.

- *extreme black* - An even deeper black with no yellow evident regardless of age.

- *chocolate* - Dark, rich brown with brown eyes.

- *mock chocolate* - A dark, but less intense brown.

- *light mock chocolate* - A shade lighter than mock chocolate.*

- *champagne* - Light brown with a pinkish undertone, pink eyes.

- *coffee* - A softer brown like a cup of coffee with cream, dark eyes.

- *beige* - A warm shade between tan and off white, dark eyes.
- *lilac* - An almost blue coat with pink tints suggesting light purple.

- *blue* - Deep slate blue with purple shading and dark eyes.

- *silver* - Light chrome-like gray with pink eyes.

- *dove* - An even mix of blue and chocolate with dark eyes.

- *lavender* - A mix of silver and champagne with pink eyes.

- *recessive yellow* - Any shade from red to blonde or dark brown. Reds have pink eyes, blonds and dark browns or sables have dark eyes.

- *yellow* - Similar to recessive yellow, but with distinct genetic differences and may exhibit white spotting.

- *cream* - Light, slightly yellow with dark eyes.

- *albino and pink eye white* - Appear pure white, but have no pigmentation, pink eyes.

- *brown eye white* - Pure white, with pigmentation in their coats.

- *ruby eye white* - Pure white, dark ruby eyes.

* Note that it is often difficult to distinguish one chocolate-toned mouse from the other unless they are compared side by side.

The following shades are also set apart for show purposes:

- *agouti* - Golden tan with a blue undercoat. Dark hair on the back, lighter on the sides and belly. Dark eyes.

- *cinnamon* - Similar to the agouti, but the dark color on the back is more chocolate in tone.

- *blue agouti* - Each hair is dark blue at the base, progressing through shades of blue toward white at the tip.

- *argenté* - Yellow top coat with lilac undercoat.

- *silver argenté* - Banded hairs progressing from a slate blue undercoat through silver to white at the tip.

- *chinchilla* - Hairs are blue at the base, gray in the middle, tipped in black. Fox belly and dark eyes.

- *silvered* - May be completely white with no pigmentation, fully colored, colored with white tips, or banded.

Recognized Mouse Color Patterns

Show mice can also display a broad range of distinct patterns in their coats. The following are accepted for show purposes.

- *brindle* - Tiger striped from the head to the tail with less distinct stripes on the stomach.

- *roan* - A mix of white and any other color evenly distributed across the body with more white on the belly.

- *merle* - A marbled pattern of solid patches on a light base color.

- *Himalayan* - White with pink eyes and dark points at the feet, ears, nose, and tail.

- *color point beige* - Cream body similar to the Himalayan, but with darker points at the feet, ears, nose, and tail with dark eyes.

- *Siamese* - A pointed variation with larger areas of shading at the points and ruby eyes. Very similar to a Siamese cat.

- *Reverse Siamese* - Any color, but with white points at the feet, ears, nose, and tail. Often the base color is coffee.

- *Burmese* - Almost any color, but with dark points at the feet, ears, nose, and tail that are the same color as but darker than the body color.

- *Sable* - Dark on the back fading to a reddish tan hue on the underside and belly.

- *Splashed* - Mice of any color, but with dark splashes on the body.

- *Tan and Fox* - A distinctly tan, highly delineated upper color region with a lighter belly.

- *Tan* - Tan with a dark golden red underside. A definitive line marks the top color from the bottom running down the jaw, along the neck, and sides.

- *Fox* - Similar coloration to the tan, but with a pure white belly. Seen in all colors and patterns.

Recognized Mouse Markings

After color and patterning, mice are also described by specific markings like "banded" or "belted." Some markings, however, are not so clearly specific and take a practiced eye to recognize.

- *belted* - Belted and banded are similar in that both are wide, mid-section markings. Belted mice have white bands that begin on and are at their thickest point on the back. They then come down the side and around the belly, typically narrowing. In especially well-bred specimens, however, the belt is almost perfectly even.

- *banded* - A solid colored mouse with a white band at the midsection thinner on the belly and broken without connecting at the spine. May be a double band, or so wide half the body is covered.

- *piebald* - The best way to describe a piebald marking is that the pattern is like that seen on black and white Holstein cattle.

- *Dutch* - On each side of the face an oval patch begins at the front of the eye and runs back to the ear without touching the whiskers. There may be a white stripe between the facial markings beginning at the nose. Any body color is acceptable, but the spots must be clean cut.

- *broken merle* - A mouse with a coat combining roan, merle, and white patches of any color.

- *broken tan* - Mice of any color with tan on the belly and white spotting.

- *variegated* - White spotted mice, but the edges of the spots are jagged. Not to be confused with splashed, which is a color-on-color pattern.

- *rump white and colored rump* - White rump with a distinct body color. The line between the two areas should be even and well defined around the body.

- *rump black and colored rump* - Identical to the rump white, but with a black posterior section.

- *tri-color* - A mouse with three colors in any mix of splashes, spots, bandings, beltings, variegations, and colors. Most are black, brown, and white.

Recognized Rat Colors

The following are all recognized colors in fancy show rats. Amazingly, the list is even more extensive than that for fancy mice!

- *black* - Deep lustrous black that runs to the skin.

- *beige* - Warm, medium tan that is not overly dark.

- *American blue* - Deep slate blue with a pale undercoat.
- *pink-eyed white* - White with red eyes.

- *black-eyed white* - White with black eyes.

- *Russian blue* - Dark gray with a ticked, heathering effect.

- *Russian dove* - Dusty, warm gray with darker guard hairs and subtle ticked heathering.

- *Russian silver* - Pale, icy gray with faintly speckled heathering.

- *Russian beige* - Pale wheat with blue-gray heathering.

- *Mink* - Even gray brown with a blue sheen.

- *silver* - Pale, cool blue with frosting of white creating a sparkle.

- *champagne* - Light, warm sand color.
- *pearl* - Silver cream. Individual hairs tipped in gray. Belly fur and feet are pale silver gray.

- *platinum* - Pale blue gray in even tone with matching feet.

- *platinum pearl* - Even undercoat of blue cream with matching feet. Each hair is tipped in blue gray.

- *Havana* - A warm, light brown that is the color of milk chocolate.

- *black-eyed cream* - Creamy white body with no odd colored hairs or patches.

- *chocolate* - Even, rich brown with no white hairs or patches.

- *merle* - Base color is mink with distributed pattern of numerous and distinct dark spots.

- *silvered* - Silvering can be present in any coat or color. The silvered hairs have white tips, which give the coat a shimmering effect.

- *agouti* - Chestnut brown with gray undercoat and black guard hairs. Belly and feet are silver gray.

- *American blue agouti* - Overall medium slate with pale gray undercoat and dark blue guard hairs. Silver belly and feet.

- *cinnamon* - Warm russet brown with even dark ticking the length of the hair. Medium gray undercoat and light gray belly and feet.

- *cinnamon pearl* - Multiple bands of cream, blue and orange giving a gold appearance with silver guard hairs. Belly is pale silver gray.

- *fawn* - Bright orange with a pale gray undercolor. Silver guard hairs and silver-cream belly fur.

- *Russian blue agouti* - Even mixed Russian Blue and agouti with heathering and silver belly fur.

- *Platinum agouti* - Soft gray ticking over warm cream with an overall blue cast. Undercolor is a lighter blue and the belly and feet are light silver.

- *Russian fawn* - Golden orange with an even ticking of silver and silver-blue guard hairs. Belly and throat are cream.

- *Russian cinnamon* - Mixture of cream, light gold, and brown on a silver-blue base with a pale undercoat. Belly and feet are light gray.

Provisional Colors

The following colorations have been accepted for provisional show status.

- *Wheaton Point Siamese* - A bright cream coat with even but gradual shading at the saddle and hindquarters. The darkest points are at the base of the tail, on the feet, and at the nose and ears. No white should be present.

- *Russian Blue Sable Burmese* - A warm, creamy blue body with darker points and faint light speckling or heathering. There should be no suggestion of black at the points.

- *Russian Blue Wheaton Sable Burmese* - Warm gray body with ticking over a light gray body. A yellow tone to the coat is normal. There should be no suggestion of black at the points.

- *American Blue Sable Burmese* - Medium warm brown body with a suggestion of blue tones.

- *Rose Gray* - Intermingled brown guard hairs on a pearl white background create an overall light brown appearance. The belly should be white. Head spots and blazes are acceptable within set parameters.

Recognized Rat Markings

Specific markings recognized in the rat fancy include:

- *self* - All one color with no markings.

- *Berkshire* - Underside should be full white with symmetrical markings. The feet and as much as half of the tail end should be white. Head spots and blazes, if small, are acceptable.

- *English Irish* - Between the two front feet and on the chest there should be a white, well defined, equilateral triangle. All four feet and the tip of the tail should also be white.
- *American Irish* - A body of any standardized color with the lower belly, tail, tip, and feet showing white markings. On the belly, the spots should be round, even, and of moderate size with no extension to the chest or legs.

- *Variegated* - Any recognized color on the head and shoulders with a blaze or head spot present. The back should have distinct and clear spots and patches, while the underside is a clean white.

- *Dalmatian* - Numerous spots of a similar size in any recognized color on a white background.

- *Hooded* - Rats with a white body and a hood in any accepted color that covers the shoulders, chest, head, neck, and throat. There should be no break or white spots in the hood. The color continues from the center of the shoulders down to the base of the tail in an unbroken line or stripe. As much of the tail as possible should also be colored.

- *Bareback* - Any standardized color on the head, neck, shoulders, and throat with white back, sides, belly, feet, and tail.

- *Capped* - Any standardized color on the head and ears as well as the underside of the jaw and chin. The shoulders, body, feet, belly, and tail are completely white.

- *Masked* - A mask over the face in any standardized color should cover both eyes. The chin, throat, muzzle, jowls, ears, body, and tail are completely white.

- *Banded* - The feet, legs, underside, sides, neck, and jaw line should be white with a wide band of color on the back.

- *Blazed* - A blaze is a wedge-shaped, symmetrical white marking. It must start midway between the eyes and ears as a fine point and encompass the bridge of the nose, the nose itself, the whisker bed and the mouth to form a thin triangle.

- *Roan* - White hairs blended with any recognized color to create a faded or salt-and-pepper look.

- *Striped* - The legs, underside, and sides are white, creating a thick strip across the back. An inverted blaze in the shape of a V should be present, with the jaw line and underside of the head also to be white.

- *Head spot* - Clear and distinct white markings centrally placed between the eyes and ears on top of the face.

- *Downunder Berkshire* - Any recognized solid body color on top with a colored stripe down the length of a white belly. The feet and as much as half of the tail are also white.

- *Downunder Hooded* - Rats with a white body and a hood in any accepted color. The hood should cover the head, neck, throat, chest, and shoulders. A line should continue from the center of the hood at the shoulders down the spine to the base of the tail. A matching belly stripe extends from the colored chest down to and filling the area between the hind legs.

- *Downunder Hooded/Spotted* - Similar to the Downunder Hooded above, but with as many side spots as possible. The back and belly stripe should match.

- *Downunder Spotted* - Back and belly stripes in any recognized color, but as broken and spotted as possible. The appearance should be that of spotting all over the back and underside.

- *Downunder Variegated* - Any recognized color on the head and shoulders with either a head spot or blaze present. The back should have distinct and clear spots and patches in the same color. There should be a symmetrical and clean belly stripe.

Standardized Rat Color Patterns

In addition to these specifications for colors and markings, the following color patterns are also recognized in the rat fancy.

- *Siamese* - A Siamese rat's body is ivory or a medium beige with gradual and even shading. The points should be dark and located on the nose, ears, feet, and at the base of the tail.

- *Seal Point* - Similar to the Siamese above, the points should be much darker, with the body color the darker, warmer beige.

- *Russian Blue Point* - The ivory color of the body is in contrast to smokey blue-gray points with some light heathering visible.

- *American Blue Point* - An ivory rat with cool yellow to brown shaded points with a very distinct level of contrast.

- *Burmese* - The body is a medium sepia tone with darker sepia points at the feet, tail, nose, and ears.

- *Sable Burmese* - A rich, brown rat with even darker points at the feet, tail, nose, and ears.

- *Russian Blue Burmese* - A medium gray body with undertones in tan and subtle ticking. The points are deep gray and found at the feet, tail, nose, and ears.

- **Russian Blue Wheaton Burmese** - A mid-sand body with ticking in blue and some yellow tone to the coat. Light gray base coat with silvery belly and distinctly darker points.

- **American Blue Burmese** - Warm, light brown body with some suggestion of blue tones. Darker points in the same shade with a white-sliver undercoat in ideal specimens.

- **Russian Silver Point Siamese** - Ivory rat with pale, icy blue-gray points with a distinct shimmer. Some heathering is normal.

- **Black Eyed Siamese** - Medium beige body with dark points evenly shaded and black eyes.

- **Seal Point** - Medium beige body with dark seal color shading that is rich and distinct.

- **Russian Blue Point** - Bright ivory body with smokey blue gray points and light heathering. Marked contrast between the points and body color.

- **American Blue Point** - Ivory body with cool yellow to brown shading at the points. Contrast should be clear and distinct.

- **Himalayan** - White base with dark points evenly shaded. Red eyes.

- *Seal Point* - Dark seal to sepia shaded points in distinct contrast against a white body.

- *American Blue Point* - White body with cool, subdued points in a yellow / brown shading.

- *Black Eyed Himalayan* - White base with dark points and black eyes.

New Varieties - January 2014

The following varieties were recognized by the National Fancy Rat Society in January 2014.

- *apricot agouti* - Pale apricot with evenly ticked guard hairs in silver. The undercolor is ice blue with a pale cream belly color.

- *Essex capped* - A white rat with a cap of color on the top of the head and extending a short way behind the ears. The nose tip, however, should be white, and there should be a white triangle between the eyes that points to the back.

- *blue point Himalayan* - White with medium smokey blue points.

- *cinnamon chinchilla* - Light brown top color intermingled with brown guard hairs over a pearl white background. The appearance is sandy and speckled.

- *coffee* - A rich caramel to be presented in an even color with no patches or white hairs present.

- *cream agouti* - Mid-cream background with mixed mid-grey ticking fading down the sides to a pale belly. Lighter fur around the eyes and on the whisker bed.

- *marten* - A dark gray body with some light heathering. Lighter fur on the face and whisker bed, around the eyes, and behind the ears. The belly is a paler shade of gray.

- *powder blue* - A pale blue with silver base fur and a pale silver belly. The color should be even, with no white patches.

- *pink eyed ivory* - Pale creamy white with no odd colored hairs. The ears, tail, and eyes should all be pink.

- *Russian dove agouti* - A warm gray with pink ticking over a light fawn background. Some heathering, light silver belly, and gray feet.

- *Russian pearl* - Medium silver with a cream, undercolor. The majority of the hairs should be pearl tipped in gray, and the top coat has a faint metallic sheen. The belly fur is pale and creamy gray.

- *satin* - A high sheen coat of any recognized color with a metallic gloss.

- *silver agouti* - Mid-gray ticking on a pale ivory background with no hint of blue or brown. The ticking on the back fades to a belly of pale ivory. The fur on the face around the eyes and whisker bed is paler.

- *turpin* - A rat with a complex series of markings including a wide band down the back, two colored triangles from the ears to the points of the eyes, and mixed color on the back giving an appearance of sprinkling.

Chapter 3 - Buying Rats, Mice, and Dormice

Certainly rats and mice can be acquired at pet stores, although this may not be the best option. Dormice are somewhat more difficult to obtain, so I will talk about them separately.

Sources for Rats and Mice

The healthiest rats and mice will come from recognized breeders. I do not recommend that you purchase any animal on impulse, which is what often occurs with companion rodents.

While you certainly can go to the pet store and get mice or rats, the truth is that under those circumstances, the animals are probably there to be sold as food for reptiles and snakes. Little if any attention will have been paid to the animal's genetic profile, and no socialization will have occurred.

Your three best sources to find high quality breeders are:

- The American Fancy Rat and Mouse Association at www.afrma.org

- The National Mouse Club at www.thenationalmouseclub.co.uk

- The National Fancy Rat Society at www.nfrs.org

Each of these organization maintains member directories and can help you locate a breeder in your area from whom you can purchase a healthy pet.

Picking a Healthy Rat

Healthy rats have a bright and curious expression in their eyes, which should literally shine with intelligence and engagement. Rats raise their noses to sniff the air when they're interested, swiveling their ears toward sounds in their environment. A rat who comes to you and smells your fingers is definitely going to make a good companion.

Look for adult rats that feel solid to the touch. You don't want an individual that is bloated or fat, but neither do you want a bony, overly thin rat. Any rat that has a tendency to hunch over and seems lethargic or unresponsive probably isn't healthy. If a rat is afraid, it will freeze in place, but only temporarily.

Listen for any signs of respiratory disease, especially wheezing. Respiratory issues are the number one health problem in companion rats.

Although fear can cause temporary diarrhea, the rat should not have a stained or soiled bottom and the cage should not show signs of excessive excrement.

Picking a Healthy Mouse

(Note that while these tips are specific to mice, you can use some of the same observations successfully with rats.)

Don't choose the largest or smallest of the mice you are shown. Individuals that exhibit some extreme size characteristic may suffer from genetic flaws. (For this reasons, it's a good idea not to let a child pick out a mouse on their own.)

Pay particular attention to the mice that approach you. That kind of behavior indicates good socialization, as well as healthy, active curiosity and confidence.

Don't pick mice that have any kind of evident discharge from the eyes or nose. You want mice with clean, shiny coats, wide open eyes, and no breathing problems. Watch out for wheezing and sneezing. The droppings in the cage should be well formed and solid.

Pay attention to the conditions in which the animals are being kept. There should be no foul odors, and the mice should not be housed in overcrowded conditions. Each cage should be lined with fresh dry bedding, and the mice should have bowls of clean food and water.

Picking a Healthy Dormouse

All of the considerations for picking healthy mice and rats can be applied to buying a dormouse. You want to pick dormice that are active and alert with no sign of discharge, respiratory issues, or external parasites.

Recommended Purchase Age

The best adoption age for mice is five weeks; for a rat, six weeks; and for a dormouse, one month. At this age, the animals can live independent of their mothers and should be well-socialized and receptive to handling and interaction.

One or Two?

Both rats and mice will be much happier living in pairs or small groups. Rodents are social creatures. They will get lonely and bored without friends of their own kind. This can lead either to aggression, or to severe lethargy.

The care profile for two companion rodents is not significantly higher. For mice, go with two females of the same size. They will be more gentle, and their urine has a less intense odor. Also, female mice live a little longer.

Male mice living together may show territorial aggression to the point of fighting. If you decide to house males, make sure they are littermates that have never been separated. Don't try introducing a new male into a habitat with an

existing male unless you want to find out just how nasty mice can be when they fight.

Now, as for rats? Males make better pets. They're more sedentary and they love to sit on your lap. Males may urine mark, but this can easily be corrected by having the animals neutered.

Female rats do make good pets, but they are much more active — to the point of often not settling down to be petted. If you have a vision of your rat riding around on your shoulder, you'll be better off with a male.

Determining Gender

The easiest way to explain the appearance of the genital area of female rats and mice is to look for two opens. The one nearest the body will resemble a "dash," while the one near the tail forms an "O."

In males, the openings are both circular. After about 14 weeks of age, the scrotum and testicles will be clearly visible, making the identification foolproof.

Given the prolific breeding capacity of rats and mice, if the animals are kept in mixed populations and you purchase a female of more than 6 weeks of age, she's likely already pregnant.

Bringing Your New Pets Home

Both mice and rats are easy to transport. Depending on where your purchase your new pets, you may bring them home in a simple cardboard box with a secure lid or even a small plastic "pet keeper" with a handle and cover. These units are inexpensive and handy, selling for about $10-$20 / £6-£12.

The first trip home for both rats and mice will be stressful, so be sensitive and allow your pets time to get used to their new surroundings and explore. Mice will need at least 24 hours to really get settled in before you should try handling and interaction. Rats, especially those that are well socialized, often need only an hour or so.

Place the travel container in the main habitat and let the little creatures emerge on their own to survey their new quarters. Do not take rats or mice out of their travel container while you are driving home. The creatures don't know you yet and can be extremely difficult to retrieve if they get away from you.

Especially with mice, be careful not to "loom" over the habitat. Keep your distance and speak softly until the mice are accustomed to the sound of your voice.

Both rats and mice are curious and engaged by nature, so be sure to place their habitat in a part of the house where there's a lot of activity. Your pets won't like being stuck off in a room by themselves. Do be careful, however, to limit all loud noises in the beginning.

With pet rodents, I prefer to put my hand in the habitat and let the title animals climb up on their own. Well-socialized rats will do this immediately, and mice learn to get "on board" quickly, especially if you offer them a little treat as an inducement.

Mice and rats are territorial, and they will like knowing that their habitat is their home base, but particularly with rats, once they're moved into their own "room," they would far prefer to spend the bulk of their time with you!

Chapter 4 - Daily Care

Rodents are attractive as pets for many reasons, not the least of which are their low maintenance needs and minimum habitat requirements. That being said, however, there are essentials that form the foundation of responsible husbandry for these little creatures. All of the following are essentials.

Mice: Selecting a Habitat

There are three standard choices for housing most rodents: aquariums, wire cages, and some sort of "habitrail" arrangement. The primary considerations with each are security, ventilation, and ease of cleaning.

An Aquarium with a "Topper"

It's not unusual to see mice, due to their small size, kept in 20-gallon / 75.7 liter aquariums. The tanks provide more than enough room for 2 mice, but are somewhat harder to keep clean and must be monitored against a build-up of toxic ammonia from soiled bedding. Also, due to the decreased ventilation from the solid glass sides, it's easy for your pets to become overheated.

Many enthusiasts take a middle ground position and outfit a 10-gallon / 37.8 liter aquarium with a wire "topper." The wire piece snaps in place and allows for the creation of a vertical habitat with different levels and interesting features like ramps and ledges for intellectual stimulation.

Toppers are typically offered as kits that may include other items for habitat augmentation. An example is the Super Pet My First Home Tank Topper package available from drsfostersmith.com.

For $33 / £20, the box includes a 10-gallon / 37.8 liter aquarium, wire topper, 3 shelves, 2 ramps, a food dish, water bottle, and a nest box.

If you go with a basic 20-gallon / 75.7 liter lidded aquarium the cost will be around $40 / £24, but you will have to acquire all the additional items separately.

Wire Cages

Wire cages do offer better ventilation and are often easier to clean because they have bottom trays that slide out. When used with rodents, wire cages must have solid plastic floors to protect your pets' feet. Expect to spend $35 to $100 (£21-£61) per cage depending on size and features.

For mice, and dormice the mesh or bars of the cage should be no more widely spaced than .25 inch / 0.5 cm. That's roughly enough room for an adult's index finger to fit between the bars.

Habitrails

Hagen Corporation manufactures a line of modular habitats under the product name "Habitrail." The interconnecting pieces allow the structure to be expanded and rearranged over time to create an environment that more naturally mimics how a rodent would live in the wild.

Habitrails are especially fun for children because they offer maximum visibility to watch all of your pets' comings and goings. The individual pieces are all ventilated, and easily snap apart for washing, but the environment is, by design, more complicated, and thus harder to maintain.

Most people feel that the high interest level is a good trade-off for having to do just a bit more maintenance. Starter kits for a Habitrail are priced at about $35 to $50 (£21-£31).

Travel Carrier

A small travel carrier is always a good idea with any kind of companion rodent. Pet stores sell simple plastic boxes with vented lids and handles that are appropriate for all kinds of small "pocket" pets as temporary transport.

An advantage of boxes of this type is that they come in a variety of sizes, and are inexpensive, typically retailing for $10-$20 / £6-£12.

Having one of these units on hand will not only allow you to safely transport your pets, but will also give you a safe place to let them "hang out" when you clean their cage.

Any time you take your rats or mice anywhere, even just a quick trip to the vet, don't leave them in the car for any length of time unless the air conditioner or heater is running. Both rats and mice tolerate some degree of cold, but little animals overheat quickly with deadly consequences.

(Unless it is absolutely necessary to do so, do not transport your dormice outside of their habitat. They are highly skilled escape artists and almost impossible to retrieve.)

Be very careful not to position the carrier in direct sunlight even if the AC is running. The sun will cause the interior temperature of the box to rise much more quickly than you realize. Often the safest place for the travel box is in the well between the front and back seats.

Rats: Extra Habitat Considerations

Most of the observations I've already made about habitats for mice also hold true for rats, with the exception of the

Habitrail. It's quite common to see enthusiasts in discussion forums complaining that they have invested in one of these set-ups only to discover that their rats don't fit through the tunnels.

Habitrails really are designed primarily for mice, hamsters, and gerbils. This doesn't mean that you can't develop the same level of interesting complexity for your rats. There are all kinds of products to create tunnels and mazes for animals as large as ferrets.

Your rat enclosure may require more forethought and planning on your part, but that's actually one of the fun things about keeping rats as pets. You'll enjoy designing their habitat creatively, and they'll enjoy living in it!
In terms of size, a cage for two rats should be, at minimum 14" x 24" and 12" high (35.56 cm x 60.96 cm x 30.48 cm) The standard rule of thumb is the bigger the better. Buy what you can afford, what you have room to place in your home, and what you don't mind cleaning.

Wire cages are highly popular for rats due to the good ventilation they offer and the opportunity they create to secure various climbing options.

Make sure that the cage floor is solid, at least in part, to protect your pets' feet from sores. If mesh is present, it should be no more than 1" x .5" (2.54 cm x 1.27 cm) for adult rats and .5" x .5" (1.27 cm x 1.27 cm) for baby rats.

The bottom pan in the cage should be about 2" / 5.08 cm deep to ensure that not too much litter is kicked out. Rat urine is highly corrosive to metal, so coated cages work best, with plastic trays in the bottom that can be replaced from time to time.

Aquariums are an option with rats, but the minimum size is 20-gallons / 75.7 liters. If you decide to go with this option, consider using a small fan to keep a steady stream of air moving across the top of the tank in hot weather.

Also, be aware that your rats may chew on the silicon sealant in the corners of the tank. This behavior does not seem to cause the rats any harm, but it often worries new rodent owners.

Rats will climb all over a wire cage, but they will rarely jump out of an aquarium. Still, for your pets' safety, it's best to use a screened top if you are keeping them in an aquarium.

Dormice: Extra Habitat Considerations

Because dormice are so active, they have slightly different housing needs in terms of spatial orientation, requiring a more vertical habitat that reflects their natural tree-dwelling lifestyle.

Regardless of the kind of enclosure you choose, it must be highly secure. Dormice are skilled escape artists and can squeeze through the tiniest crack. For this reason, glass tanks really are the best option.

Two dormice can live comfortably in a 20-gallon / 75.7 liter tank, but it should have plenty of branches of various sizes for climbing, as well as suspended ropes, and a selection of nest boxes.

Many enthusiasts use finch nests that are sold for use in bird cages and place several of them around in the habitat. Dormice love to snuggle in and feel secure. These small bamboo houses create perfect hideaways and cost less than $10 / £6 each.

Considering Custom Cages

These ready-made options are certainly not the only kind of habitat used with companion rodents. I strongly advise going online and using your favorite search engine to look for "custom rat cage" (or mouse or dormouse cage).

All of the major search engines give you an option to look at photos that match your search term. This is an excellent way to browse cages designed by rodent enthusiasts, and to get ideas for building or commissioning your own custom cage.

Since mice, rats, and dormice are happiest when kept in groups, and are in constant need of intellectual stimulation, the more room you can provide your pet and the more interesting the configuration of their home, the more they will thrive.

Observations on Cage Placement

As I mentioned in the previous chapter, most pet rodents like to be in parts of the house where there's plenty of activity going on.

Mice are more sensitive to noise, and should certainly be kept well away from blaring stereos or TVs. To some degree this is also true of rats, but many owners say they find their rats actually watching the television set.

Dormice are the exception to this rule since they are nocturnal and will be sound asleep during the day. Put

---

their cage in a quiet room during the daylight hours, but also find a spot where you can enjoy watching them play in the evening.

Position the cage on a table or some sort of stand well away from drafts, and make sure that any other pets in the house cannot gain access to the habitat or topple it over. Don't place a rodent or any other small caged animal near a window. Direct sunlight can cause rapid overheating and death.

Although pet rodents can be quite noisy at night, rats in particular need a period of complete darkness each day. If they are exposed to too much light on a regular basis, pet rats have a tendency to develop tumors. Close the curtains, and don't use a night light in the same room with your rats.

Temperature Considerations

Mice should be kept in a temperature range of 65 - 80 F / 18.3 - 26.6 C. They have no specific requirements for humidity, but if the levels get too high, it's an indication the enclosure isn't getting enough ventilation or that the bedding is damp and in need of changing.

If you mice are overheated, they'll go into a corner and start to hyperventilate rather than try to drink more water. The result is very rapid dehydration followed by death if their temperature isn't lowered quickly.

Rats will do fine down to 65 F / 18.3 C and will be uncomfortable in temperatures above 90 F / 32.2 C. The optimum level is 70 F to 75 F (21.1 C to 23.8 C) with a relative humidity of 50%.

Rats release excess heat from their bodies through their tails. You can tell how hot the animal is by feeling the tail. Rats that are experiencing heatstroke will drool, exhibit lethargic behavior, and finally slip into unconsciousness. (To learn more about heatstroke in mice and rats, see the chapter on health.)

Dormice should be kept at 70 F / 21.1 C. At temperatures of 65 F / 18.3 C or lower, dormice may start to hibernate, which is very dangerous for captive animals that aren't physically prepared to go through the process. A relative humidity between 30% and 70% will be fine for dormice.

Regardless of the kind of rodent you are keeping, install a digital thermometer inside your pet's habitat. These units are easily purchased at pet stores or online. Fluker's makes a reliable and fairly priced Digital Display Thermo-Hygrometer for $20 / £12.

Choosing a Substrate and Bedding

Substrate considerations are fairly equal for all of these creatures. Avoid cedar and pine shavings. The phenols in these products create serious health problems for small pets including liver disease, respiratory issues, and suppression of the immune system.

Ground corn cobs and shredded newspapers are good options for mice, but avoid the use of corn cobs with rats.

They tend to eat the material and it gets caught in their throats, raising the potential for choking.

Due to the widespread use of soya-based inks, newspaper is safe, but the ink still rubs off on your pet's fur and creates the need for additional grooming unless you purchase recycled paper processed into pellets.
Some examples of commercial litters include:

Kaytee Kay-Kob Litter
8 lbs. / 3.6 kg
$13 / £7.8

Mountain Meadows Pet Products
Critter Country Small Animal and Reptile Bedding
20 lbs. / 9.07 kg
$26 / £15.67
(Made of wheat grass.)

Yesterday's News
Softer Texture Fresh Scent Cat Litter
26.4 lbs. / 11.97 kg
$14 / £8.45
(Made from recycled newspaper.)

Nest Boxes

Rats, mice, and especially dormice enjoy curling up in bedding. Small hanging bird baskets are excellent for dormice, and commercial nest boxes are perfect for mice and rats because they disassemble for ease of cleaning.

Get nest boxes that are big enough for two or more animals to curl up together — because they will — and put them up on a ledge off the floor of the habitat. Rats are perfectly happy with just about any old cardboard box, although they may gnaw the box to shreds in no time.

Hay, grass, or alfalfa makes excellent bedding and you can also use yarn, cotton, or cloth although these latter materials are not appropriate for use with babies who can get their heads tangled in the loose threads. Felt and fleece are safe, and commercial corn husk bedding is also an option.

Cage Maintenance

The primary consideration with cage maintenance is to control odor that is unpleasant for you and potentially deadly for your pets. Accumulations of ammonia in rodent cages create fumes that will irritate the lining of your pets' lungs making them more susceptible to viral and bacterial infections.

The larger the cage you provide for your pets, the more slowly ammonia will build up, and the better your chances of staying ahead of soiling with daily spot cleaning. Both mice and rats have a tendency to pick one corner of their cage as a designated "bathroom," which makes your job much easier.

(Even when rats and mice are loose outside their habitat, they will typically go back inside the cage if possible to "do their business.")

Once a week you should remove all the litter from the habitat and wipe the base down with a solution of half water / half vinegar. Use the same cleaner on all exposed surfaces, making sure everything is dry before you return your pets to their "apartment."

On a monthly basis take the entire habitat apart and wash it down thoroughly in the bathtub, or even outside where you can hose everything off and allow the components to dry in the sun and air out.

The Matter of Escapes

There is no set method for dealing with escapes. Mice are extremely territorial by nature. Typically once they've come to see their habitat as their "kingdom," they don't try to get out. Single mice that are bored or lonely are much more likely to "make a break for it" than mice living in pairs or groups.

Many rat owners allow their pets some degree of free ranging activity because rats can be taught to come when called, and in general prefer to be close to their humans. Therefore, with rats, it's less an issue of them escaping and more that you've lost track of your pet.

Dormice should never be given an opportunity to get out. They are lightning fast and almost impossible to catch once they're beyond the confines of their "world."

Any time you allow a pet rodent access to an area, you want to plug all possible holes, including those in the furniture. Escaped mice and rats can easily find their way into couches or recliners and suffer serious injury of death.

If you have an escaped rodent, try moving the habitat into the area where you believe the animal is hiding. In most cases, the rat or mouse will ultimately return to their home base. You can also try putting out favorite treats to lure hiding pets into the open.

I personally think that the best way of dealing with an escape is to simply prevent it in the first place. Don't let mice or rats free range in a large area. If you want to give them time out of the cage, rodent proof a small room and stay with your pets, observing them at all times. Rats will happily ride around on their humans, and they will even agree to being put on a leash with a harness.

If your rat does go "walk about" in the house, he's exploring rather than trying to get away. Don't be surprised if he comes and finds you on the couch or in the bed.

(If you are interested in harness training your rat, look for a product like the Ware Nylon Walk-N-Vest Pet Harness and leash. The small version should fit most pet rats. The item retails for less than $10 / £6.)

Diet and Nutrition

The popular perception is that mice and rats invade storage pantries at will and eat everything in sight. If you take this approach to feeding your pets, you'll have obese rodents with very short lifespans.

Feeding Your Mouse

In order to provide balanced nutrition with appropriate caloric intake, give your mice a formulated pellet food with a good mixture of carbohydrates, protein, vitamins, and minerals. These might include:

Mazuri Rodent Pellets
2 lbs / .9 kg
$6 / £3.6
Purina Garden Recipe Rat & Mouse Diet
4 lbs / 1.8 kg
$11 / £6.67

Kaytee Forti-Diet Pro Health - Mouse, Rat & Hamster
3 lbs / 1.4 kg

$5.79 / £3.5

Don't choose a food with seeds as they are lower in quality and more prone to fungal growth.

Keep your pets' bowl filled at all times. Mice need a constant source of food and will nibble throughout the day.

Your mice can have nuts (like pecans and walnuts), fruits, and vegetables as treats, but don't let these items account for more than 20% of the overall food intake. Acceptable choices include:

- carrots
- corn on the cob
- bell peppers
- green beans
- squash
- sweet potato
- green leafy vegetables

The sugar content in fruits is high, so offer the following in limited quantities.

- cherries
- melons
- bananas
- apples
- blueberries
- strawberries

If you can afford to do so, purchase organic produce and wash all items thoroughly to minimize the chance that your pets are exposed to herbicides or insecticides.

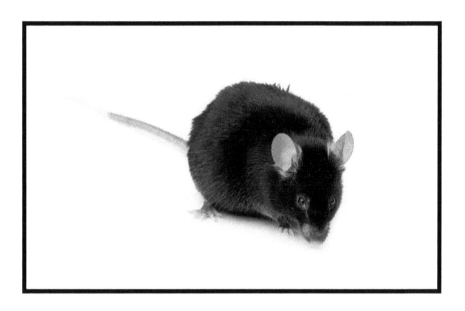

If you would peel an item before eating it, the same should be done for your pet. Offer all vegetables to your mice raw to help keep your pets' teeth worn down. Avoid all canned vegetables, which are high in salt and also contain preservatives and harmful chemicals like dyes.

There are definitely foods that you don't want to give your pets, including:

- avocadoes
- citrus fruits (cause diarrhea)
- garlic and onions (cause anemia)
- cheese (causes gastrointestinal distress)
- chocolate (contains toxic theobromine)

- peanut butter (choking hazard)

The best rule of thumb to follow is to not give your mice "human" food. Keep them on well-formulated pellets, and don't overfeed.

Feeding Your Rat

Rats also benefit for a low-calorie diet that combines rodent blocks with fruits, vegetables, and legumes. Although many rat owners do feed a mix of seeds and grains, you'll see a lot of waste with that approach. Rats can be highly particular, picking out only what they like and ignoring the rest.

Also, many mixed foods contain rabbit pellets, which rats don't digest well. For this reason, rodent blocks are more nutritionally sound, and more cost effective in terms of cutting down on waste.

Products like Oxbow Regal Rat Food are both affordable and healthy for your pets. A 3 lb. / 1.36 kg bag retails for $14 / £8.44. The pellets contain 15% crude protein with just 4% crude fat. The primary ingredients are brown rice, oats, wheat, soy, and fish meal.

This will give your rat all the proper dietary components, especially when offered with supplemental fresh foods like broccoli, kale, sweet potatoes, bok choy, tomatoes, and cooked beans.

Feeding Your Dormouse

As mentioned earlier, the most popular dormice in the pet trade are African Pygmy Dormice. They are omnivores, which makes feeding them easy in one regard, but you must strive for a diet that is both fresh and varied.

Always make multiple food items available in the enclosure, and place them in separate bowls to entice your pets to sample different foods throughout the day.

Seeds, grains, and nuts are all acceptable, leading many dormice owners to use various birdseed mixes with their pets. Hamster and gerbil foods that contain sunflower seeds or raw peanuts are also a good dietary staple.

Mix this content with fresh fruits and vegetables as well as nectar (also a companion bird dietary product.) Feed live crickets and mealworms (sold in pet stores for use with pet reptiles) as a source of protein along with hard boiled eggs, cooked chicken, and yogurt.

Offer your dormice a seed mixture in the morning. Experiment with how much your pets will consume in a day, and don't practice a policy of free feeding. Your dormice will fill up on the seeds and nuts and ignore their other foods.
Give fresh items (including protein sources) in the evening, removing the uneaten bits the next morning.

Hydration

Mice, rats, and dormice all need a constant supply of clean, fresh, de-chlorinated water. Use a hanging water bottle with a ball bearing tip like those made by Lixit.

This method of dispensing water prevents your pets' bedding from getting soaked while keeping the water itself clean of debris. Water bottles also give you an accurate means to determine if your pets are drinking enough.

An 8 ounce / 0.23 liter hanging bottle sells for about $5 / £3. Always change the water daily and test the tip of the bottle to ensure the liquid flows freely.

Good hydration helps pet rodents to maintain their body temperature while keeping their system flushed free of toxins. Don't allow their water to become stale or stagnant, as this increases the chances of dangerous bacterial growth.

Toys and Intellectual Stimulation

All pet rodents are, by nature, busy little creatures. They are always curious, on the go, and gnawing on something! Toys, especially boxes and tunnels, and climbing structures will all be a huge hit.

Not all item have to be purchased. Mice and rats will happily chew on old fiber egg cartons or cardboard tubes. Any chew toy that is rated as safe for either a small rodent or a bird is perfectly fine — and there are literally thousands of choices!

Almost all toys that are suitable for pet rodents are inexpensive, falling in a $3-$10 / £1.8-£6 price range. Just make sure that you buy plenty of toys made of good dense wood. Rodents' incisors are always growing and need to be kept worn down.

Definitely include a solid running wheel. The plastic tracks are much safer for your pets' paws than the old style with rungs. Get the smallest size, around 4.5 inches / 11.43 cm for mice and dormice, and a larger size for rats. Depending on size, running wheels cost $8-$15 / £5-£9.

Bathing

You will only rarely be concerned with bathing your pet rats, as they are naturally very fastidious animals.

Occasionally if a rat overheats, submerging your pet up to its neck in cool (not cold) water is an effective way to help your pet lower its temperature. Otherwise, there is no need to bathe your rat.

Mice don't need to be bathed either, but, unlike rats and dormice, they will enjoy a dust bath from time to time, which is a great way to remove excessive dirt and oil from their coats.

Offer your pet mice a shallow bowl of Chinchilla Dust Bath (2.5 lbs. / 1.13 kg / $10 / £6) for about half an hour once a week. Your mice will know exactly what to do! Always take the dish out of the habitat when your mice are finished, and clean up any dust that has been spilled or scattered.

(To save yourself some time and effort, offer your mice their dust bath on the same day when you plan to give their cage its weekly cleaning.)

Training Your Pets

Both rats and mice are used in scientific studies on behavior and psychological responses because they are highly intelligent and skilled at solving puzzles.
Pet rodents don't play in the same way dogs and cats might, but they catch on very quickly and are highly receptive to extrapolating actions and behaviors into more complex sequences.

In the beginning, I recommend just watching what your pets do naturally and building on those behaviors. Rats are very good with language, easily learning their names and picking up working vocabularies, so definitely talk to your pets and use "command" words consistently.

Since you don't want to overfeed your pets, don't rely completely on treats to reinforce desired behaviors. Both rats and mice will enjoy being praised, and you can always use small bits of their regular diet — seeds, nuts, or a bit of fruit as edible rewards.

Don't ever speak loudly to your pets. The only "negative" reinforcement should be just ignoring the "mistake," and trying again. I encourage rodent owners not to get locked into some set routine. Have fun with your pet! Cater to his natural inclinations as you get to know one another and let all "tricks" develop spontaneously.

Dormice are less "trainable" because they are, by nature, rather skittish. It is not impossible to hand train a dormouse, but the socialization must begin at an early age and does not work equally well for all individuals.

When dormice are receptive to being handled, they are less likely to want to be held than to climb all over you. Always make sure that you are interacting with your dormice in a secure area with as little chance of escape as possible!

Chapter 5 - Health and Breeding

For the most part, there's little that can be done to treat conditions in pet mice other than respiratory infection, external parasites, and broken bones. Mice are too small and fragile to really benefit from much in the way of preventive health care. Their best "insurance" is excellent husbandry.

Rats are somewhat more receptive to medical care and can be successfully spayed and neutered. In both cases, however, owners do need to educate themselves about the possible health issues that will arise with their pets.

Often, it's difficult to find a vet with extensive experience treating companion rodents, especially when you're dealing with something as unusual as a dormouse.

(This chapter primarily discusses known health issues in mice and rats, but all of these problems can be present in dormice as well. Again, however, these creatures are relatively rare in the pet trade. They, like all small rodents, are at the greatest danger from tumors and respiratory infections.)

If you have no access to an exotic vet, the best you may be able to hope for is a small animal vet who is willing to listen to you, and to consult with other vets and learn what is best for your companion rodent. Either way, much of the responsibility for your pets' wellbeing rests squarely with you.

Observe Your Pets Carefully

Really for almost any kind of pet, an observant human is the strongest of all health guards. You, more than anyone, will know what is "normal" for your pet. If you think something is wrong with your mouse or rat, it probably is. There are, of course, signs that can be taken as red flags for the presence of potential illness:

- Weight loss or gain, especially if the change is sudden and dramatic and not in response to any alteration in diet.

- A reluctance to move or difficulty in doing so. If your pet is limping, or walking in an unsteady or uneven way, be concerned.

- Changes in the quality of the coat that make it look uneven or dingy, including self-injury from excessive or frequent scratching. Also look for any kind of wound, abrasion, or skin discoloration.

- A hunched over sitting posture with the abdomen tucked up. This behavior may or may not be accompanied by poorly formed stools and soiling of the anal area. A distended abdomen is also a reason for alarm.

- Any growth, bump, or lump, especially those that have come on suddenly and appear to be changing rapidly.

- Discharge and crusty accumulation at the nostrils or eyes, as well as cloudiness of the eye and squinting.

- Grinding of the teeth and any indication that your pet is not able to eat comfortably, like drooling or holding the head to one side when eating.

- Any sign of respiratory distress including raspy or wheezy breathing, sneezing, and chattering.

Be careful not to engage in any negligent husbandry practices that can contribute to ill health including poor diet, over-crowding, and allowing ammonia fumes to build up in the habitat.

Understanding Prophyrin

First-time rat owners are often panicked when they see a red discharge under their pet's eyes. Rats have a red pigment in their tears called prophyrin that is often mistaken for blood.

A small amount of this pigmentation is nothing to worry about. If, however, the amount seems excessive and has spread to other areas of the face, your rat may have either an eye problem or a respiratory infection and should be evaluated by a veterinarian.

Common Illnesses and Health Problems

The following health issues are the ones most commonly seen in pet rats and mice. Some problems can be corrected by improved husbandry, while others will require veterinary treatment. Unfortunately, in many cases, your only recourse will be palliative care to make your pet more comfortable.

Respiratory Infections

Respiratory infections are the primary leading cause of death in pet mice and rats. If your pet chatters constantly and is wheezing, an infection is the most likely culprit.

When one or more rodents are housed together, the infected pet should be quarantined immediately to protect the others. The leading causes of a respiratory infection are mycoplasmosis, secondary bacterial infections, and congestive heart failure. Rats can also have a strep infection, which, if untreated, is typically fatal within three days.

If you have strep throat, you should not handle your rats or be in the room with them, as you can pass the infection to your pets. Rats can also have infections of the inner ear that seriously disrupt their balance or damage it permanently if the condition is left unaddressed. Antibiotics and steroids are immediately indicated.

In both rats and mice, oral antibiotics can be administered with an eyedropper or with a syringe from which the needle has been removed.

One of the best safeguards against respiratory infection is to make sure ammonia does not build up in your pets' habitat. The fumes will damage and weaken their lungs and make them more susceptible to infection.

Growths, Lumps, and Tumors

Tumors and abscesses are the second leading cause of death in companion rodents. When a growth is detected, your vet will first try to determine if it is an abscess that can be drained and treated with antibiotics. Abscesses begin to shrink in a few days, but tumors will refill with fluid. Other symptoms of cancer include:

- An area of ulcerated skin.
- A lump that bleeds persistently.
- Distention of the abdomen.
- Sudden and marked weight loss.
- Lethargic behavior.

(Please note that dental abscesses are particularly serious. Any lumps or growths on the jaws require immediate attention.)

Mammary gland tumors are the cancers most commonly seen in mice and rats, with metastasis to lungs. Contrary to popular belief, however, rats and mice are no more prone to suffering from cancer than any other animal. That association has built up in the common consciousness because these animals are used so widely for research purposes.

In some cases, cancers can be treated with tamoxifen, which can extend your pet's life by 2-3 months. In most cases where tumors are left untreated, death occurs within 2-3 weeks. Often the short-term gain and the high cost of treatment leads owners to opt for the most humane action, which is likely euthanasia.

Excessive Scratching

Usually when a rat or mouse scratches constantly and injuries themselves as a result, an external parasite like lice or mites are present. These pests can be treated with ivermectin or pyrethrin, but the dosage must be correctly prescribed by a vet. Additionally, the habitat must be cleaned and disinfected, with all bedding completely discarded.

In cases of severe self-injury, glove your pet's hind feet with tiny bits of masking tape carefully folded over to allow for movement, but not wounding.

Over a course of 2-3 weeks both the habitat and your pet may need to be treated again. The trick in eradicating parasites is always to stay ahead of the next batch of hatching eggs. This can take time, and certainly requires diligent attention.

Diarrhea

As is often the case, any treatment with antibiotics in companion animals like mice and rats can lead to diarrhea. The drugs cure one illness, but they also kill the flora in the gut, leading to an overgrowth of bacteria. Often in these cases simply adding a probiotic like acidophilus to your pet's food will quickly restore proper digestive function.

Diarrhea may also be caused by imbalanced electrolytes that are a consequence of poor nutrition. In this case a vet will need to prescribe a fluid supplement to restore the correct levels and any new or unusual foods will need to be immediately discontinued.

Bumblefoot

Bumblefoot is a bacterial infection that attacks the bottom of the heel, and can occur in any animal housed in a cage with a wire mesh bottom. The area becomes swollen and red with a crusty yellow scab forming that can break open and bleed.

Although a vet may prescribe a topical ointment to ease the discomfort and lessen further infection, the best treatment is to remove the source of the irritation by covering the body of the cage with a soft mat or even a plastic needlepoint canvas.

Ringworm

"Dermatophytosis" or ringworm is a fungal skin infection that causes a crusty open wound with severe itching leading to excess scratching.

An accurate diagnosis of ringworm requires that the area be cultured. Treatment is with a topical medication, and until the infection clears, you will need to wear gloves when handling your pets.

Swelling of the Abdomen

Swelling and distention of the abdomen typically means the rodent is suffering from lymphoma or leukemia. Other indications may be hard and swollen lymph nodes and shallow breathing. (Of course, in females, the chance of pregnancy must also be excluded.)

Nothing can be done to help a rodent with lymphoma or leukemia. Both conditions are extremely painful, so euthanasia is recommended.

Old Age

As rats and mice age, the problems they exhibit can rarely be addressed by more than kind care. These include, but are not limited to kidney failure and dental misalignments.

As with all elderly pets, providing good quality food and water and a warm place to curl up and sleep are great kindnesses. The shorter lifespan of rats and mice when compared to dogs and cats is something the all rodent enthusiasts must accept.

Keeping your little friend comfortable and loving them to the end of their lives is simply part of the "deal." You may be surprised at how difficult it is to say good-bye to these winsome little creatures. They are so personable and so beguiling that far from being "throw away" pets, they are a strong and vital presence in the life of their humans and genuinely mourned in the end.

Zoonotic Diseases

A disease is said to be zoonotic when it can be passed from an animal to a human. This is not a problem in domesticated rodents, but wild colonies of rats and mice can harbor dangerous viruses and bacteria including, but not limited to:

- salmonella
- lymphocytic choriomeningitis virus (LCM)
- leptospira
- giardia
- cryptosporidia
- various skin fungi

The presence of these microorganisms is due to the highly enclosed nature of the wild colonies where feces and urine accumulate in large quantities. Individuals at the greatest risk of contracting a zoonotic disease are children, the elderly, and those with compromised immune systems.

Spaying and Neutering

Typically mice and dormice are not spayed because they are so very small, although males can be successfully neutered. These surgeries are far more common in rats, offering both health and behavioral benefits.
In rats, spaying and neutering reduces the incidence of mammary tumors, but also pituitary tumors which, when present, are consistently fatal. It is estimated that 70% of unspayed female rats will develop one or the other of these tumors, but they are present in only 4% of spayed rats.

Female rats should be spayed between 3-6 months of age when they are not in heat.

Neutering a male rat will stop urine-marking and help to curb aggressive behavior, while also lowering the risk of testicular cancer.

Breeding Companion Rodents

There is no problem breeding companion rodents, but rather in NOT breeding them! Female mice reach sexual maturity at 6-7 weeks of age, males at 7-8 weeks. Rats are sexually mature by 5 weeks of age. If you adopt a female from a mixed group beyond those ages, you can be almost certain she will be pregnant.

Fertility in Females

Female rats and mice cycle every 4-5 days! The period of fertility is short, typically about 12 hours. Breeding generally occurs at night and is not limited to any one season of the year.

It is often difficult to determine when a pair of rodents have mated. Check for the presence of a waxy, cream colored vaginal plug in the female, which will drop out into the habitat within 24 hours of mating.

The gestation period for mice is 18-21 days, for rats 21-23 days and for African Pygmy Dormice 25-28 days.

(The Common or Hazel Dormouse, indigenous to the UK, has a gestation period of 22-24 days, but you must have a license to own and breed these animals. They are primarily cultivated by conservation groups seeking to reintroduce them into the wild, and are not a part of the pet trade.)

Mice litters can number 4-15 pups. Females are capable of have 5-10 litters in any 12 month period. Each of the babies weighs 0.5-1.5 grams. It would take four mouse pups to equal the weight of one sugar cube.

Rat litters average 6-24 babies, each weighing 6-8 grams each.

African Pygmy Dormice have much smaller litters, just 2-4 pups that weigh about 3.5 grams at birth.

Should You Breed Rats, Mice, and Dormice?

If you are breeding rats, mice, and dormice as part of the rodent fancy, you will be faced with acquiring a fair amount of understanding regarding genetics to get the most desirable results. Beyond that? All there really is to breeding rodents is to put an intact mating pair in the same cage!

The things I would caution you to consider are the size of the resulting litters, the fact that overcrowding of companion rodents is cruel, and that there are already far too many unwanted animals in the world.

If you try to keep all of the pups born to your mated pairs, you will soon be overrun and it's unlikely you'll be able to maintain your husbandry standards.

Buying your pets from reputable breeders ensures that you are at no risk of unplanned litters because you can acquire same sex cage mates or, in the case of rats, have your pets spayed or neutered.

The bottom line is this, only breed companion rodents if you have the room, time, and money to care for them appropriately or if you have homes for the pups lined up *before* they are born.

Chapter 6 - An Overview of Rodent Shows

Rodent shows began in England in the 1900s and are growing in popularity today in the UK and the U.S. as a way to showcase pedigreed mice and rats while promoting the practice of keeping these animals as companions.

Rodent Show Basics

Like all shows where pedigreed animals are exhibited, individual entrants are judged according to standards of excellence formulated by the show's governing body.

To maximize participation and to give breeders as many venues as possible to compete for ribbons and "best in show" titles, animals are shown in various classes delineated by such factors as coat type, color, or marking pattern.

American Fancy Rat and Mouse Association

In the United States, the American Fancy Rat and Mouse Association (AFRMA) hosts the majority of rodent shows. The overall AFRMA's basic requirements include the following:

- Owners or an equally responsible party must show all animals.

- Although the organization will attempt to ensure the safety of all animals, it cannot be held responsible for injury, loss, or death.

- Animals must be shown in their natural condition. No alteration of color or coat quality is allowed.

- Once paid, entry fees cannot be refunded.

- Even if an animal is placed in the wrong class for its type, it will be judged in that class and all animals are subject to elimination.

- Exhibitors and judges are not allowed to engage in any discussion during the evaluation of the animals unless the contact is initiated by the judge.

- Once a judgment is rendered, the decision is final.

- Co-operation and sportsmanship are expected on the part of the exhibitors.

Judging at AFRMA shows is conducted according to the Official Standards of the American Fancy Rat and Mouse Association.

Recognized AFRMA Mouse Varieties

The AFRMA recognizes seven varieties of fancy mice by coat type:

- **Standard** - Coat is short and sleek.
- **Satin** - Short and sleek, but with a lustrous sheen.
- **Long Hair** - A coat with long, thick, fine, and silky texture.

- **Long Hair Satin** - Same as above, but with a satin sheen.
- **Frizzie** - Hair that is tightly fizzed or waved over the whole body, and dense. Whiskers are curled.
- **Frizzie Satin** - Same as above, but with a satin sheen.
- **Hairless** - No hair at all. The skin should be translucent pink, bright, thin, and with no scars or blemishes.

These varieties are then grouped into five sections ordered by markings and color.

- Mice that are uniform in color are called "self." These shades include: black, beige, blue, chocolate, coffee, cream, champagne, dove, gold, fawn, lilac, ivory, red, orange, silver, or white.

- Mice with any recognized shade as a top color and a contrasting near white underside are described as "fox." If the underside is rich and golden with red tones, the color is "tan." The dividing line must be distinct, straight, and clear, running from the jaw and down along the chest.

- The marked section has seven groups that can be associated with any recognized color. (Refer to Chapter 2 for full descriptions of acceptable markings.)

Mice can also be placed in categories for unstandardized animals and non-recognized colors.

Overall Characteristics of Show Mice

Show quality mice have slender, long bodies and clear, large eyes. They exhibit a clean profile and have expressive long, ears. Long tails that taper are also valued. The overall length of a show mouse including tail should be 8-9 inches / 20.32-22.86 cm. The mice should have a good temperament and should respond well to handling.

Recognized AFRMA Rat Varieties

The AFRMA recognizes seven varieties of fancy mice primarily by coat type:

- **Standard** - Coat is smooth, short, and glossy.
- **Rex** - The coat is curly, with curly whiskers.
- **Tailless** - No tail whatsoever is present.
- **Satin** - A longer, thinner coat with a lustrous sheen.
- **Dumbo** - Overly large ears placed on the side of the head.

Like fancy mice, these varieties are grouped into five sections for color and markings.

- Self rats are uniform in color with recognized shades including: beige, black, blue, blue-beige, champagne, chocolate, cocoa, lilac, mink, platinum, Russian blue, Russian dove, sky blue, black-eyed white, and pink-eyed white.

- Rats that are said to be AOC (any other color) are all one color but the individual hairs of the coat are

---

banded with two or more colors and there are colored guard hairs interspersed throughout. These colors include: agouti, amber, blue agouti, chinchilla, cinnamon, cinnamon pearl, fawn, lynx, pearl, and Russian blue agouti.

- Rats that are AOCP (any other color pattern) are a combination of two or more colors arranged in recognized patterns. These colors include: blue point Siamese, Burmese, Himalayan, Russian blue agouti Burmese, Russian blue point Siamese, seal point Siamese, and merle.

- Silvered rats have coats interspersed with white hairs, with the recognized colors including silver black, silver blue, silver chocolate, silver fawn, silver lilac, and silver mink.

- Marked rats include eleven types, described in Chapter 2. The designations are, English Irish, Irish.

Other classifications include odd-eye rats that have one pink eye and one that is ruby or black, and unstandardized animals as well as those with non-recognized colors and markings.

Overall Characteristics of Show Rats

Show rats should have racy, long bodies with a well-maintained weight. Their eyes should be large with a bold look, well placed in a long, clean head with large ears.

Long, tapering tails are a plus. The overall length of the body should be 8-10 inches / 20.32-25.4 cm.

The National Mouse Club

In the UK, the National Mouse Club has similar standards for show mice, which are published at TheNationalMouseClub.co.uk.

The general standard of excellence cites the following points:

- a long body
- elongated, clean head
- a nose that is not overly pointed or fine
- bold, large, and prominent eyes
- large, tulip-shaped ears free of creases
- ears held erect
- sufficient width between the ears

The overall desired appearance is described as "racy," meaning a body that is long and slim with a suggestion of arching over the loin. The tail should originate from a thick root, tapering to a fine "whiplash" point in a straight line free of any kinking. The tail and body should be of roughly equal lengths.

The National Fancy Rat Society

Like the National Mouse Club in the UK, the National Fancy Rat Society has general standards of excellence much in keeping with those it its American counterparts including:

- the rat should be of a "good size"
- a long and racy build for females
- a bigger build for males with arching over the loin
- clean, long head
- not overly pointed at the nose
- round, bold eyes
- well formed, widely spaced ears
- ears, feet, and tail covered in fine hair
- long, cylindrical tail thick at the base and tapered to a point

As with mice, the tail and body should be of roughly equal length. The coat should be fine, smooth, and glossy unless the type calls for a curled finish as in the rex.

Chapter 7 - Frequently Asked Questions

To really understand life with companion rodents, I recommend that you read the entire text. The following are, however, some of the most frequently asked questions about the behavior of these animals and the husbandry they require.

How do companion rodents behave as pets?

That depends entirely on the rodent in question. Mice are most active early in the day, as the sun is going down, and throughout the night. Rats are somewhat more amenable to adjusting to your schedule, although they do need a period of complete darkness every day.

Dormice sleep through the day and must be carefully regulated in terms of their temperature so they don't slip into their natural tendency to hibernate.

All of these animals are, by nature, very active and rarely just sitting around doing nothing. Rodents are constantly engaged and on the go, investigating, eating, grooming, gnawing — basically doing all the things that make them what they are.

Of the three, rats are the most intelligent, but mice and dormice run them a close second. Dormice are the most hyperactive and the least responsive to handling as a result, but all rodents recognize and respond to kindness and gentle handling. Rats and mice in particular will greet you affectionately and with enthusiasm and happily climb on to your hand.

Can wild rodents be tamed and made pets?

While it is not impossible to tame wild rats, mice, and dormice, it is rarely advisable to attempt doing so. (In the UK, it's illegal to own and breed wild dormice without a license.)

Wild rodents really never settle down in captivity. They will always be more nervous. Domesticated rats and mice are just that — domesticated. They are the product of selective breeding to cultivate the best traits of companion animals including docility and receptivity to handling.

Feeder mice are cheap. Do they make good pets?

While feeder mice can make good pets, they are typically born into and kept in absolutely horrible conditions. It is very rare for any care to be taken about their health because basically from the moment of their birth, their fate as reptile food is pretty well sealed.

While I fully understand the urge to rescue the little animals from their ultimate demise, don't expect feeder mice to live as long or to be as healthy as fancy mice. They, like all rodents, will respond to love and attention, but they are not the best option for pets.

Why do fancy rats and mice make better pets?

Fancy rats and mice are the product of planned breeding programs. They are well cared for from the moment of birth and will come to you well socialized and very tame, both by nature and by experience.

Also, with fancy rodents you will have more choices to pick color, markings, and coat type. These are gorgeous little creatures and they make attractive and appealing pets.

Do dormice make good pets?

Dormice are very interesting pets to watch, but they aren't as tame or as agreeable to handling as mice and rats. (They are also very tiny, so handling them can cause injury unless you are very careful.)

You also have to be more vigilant about preventing escapes. For this reason, they aren't really suitable pets for children unless an adult is actively involved in the husbandry routine.

What is the projected lifespan of each of these animals?

Both rats and mice have a lifespan of 2 to 2.5 years, with rats generally surviving the longest. Dormice are the longest lived of the three, often surviving four years.

Are rats, mice, and dormice hypoallergenic?

No, in fact companion rodents are responsible for as many or more allergic reactions in humans than dogs and cats. If you are worried about the potential of such a reaction, get tested before you adopt one of these pets!

Are rats, mice, and dormice good pets for children?

Children of more than 9 years of age, with proper instruction, and supervision from adults can typically care for rats and mice. They must, however, understand how to handle their pets, and they must be responsible about feeding and habitat maintenance.

Dormice are not good pets for children. They are small, fragile, quite hyperactive, and almost impossible to catch once they escape.

How many rats, mice, or dormice should I get at one time?

All rodents are social animals. It's best to keep at least a pair, otherwise your pets will get bored, depressed, and even aggressive. A rat can live alone if you are prepared to spend most of your time fulfilling your pet's need for companionship, but single mice tend to be really problematic because they will work harder to escape simply to find something to do!

Should I adopt males or female rodents?

Same gender pairings work best to avoid unplanned litters unless you decide to have the male of the pair neutered, which is a viable option with rats. Mice and dormice are really too small to do well with the surgery.

For smaller rodents, two females of the same age and size will do quite well together. Unaltered male rodents often have issues with territorial aggression unless they are litter mates that have never been separated.

How can you distinguish gender in companion rodents?

The best way in very young rodents is to examine the two anal openings. In males, both openings are round. In females, the one nearest the body is a slit. As the animals age, the scrotum and testicles on males are clearly visible, making identification simple.

Are pet rodents hard work?

Obviously all animals require a commitment on your part to feed and care for them, maintain their habitat, and interact with them. On a daily basis, rodent habitats should be spot cleaned, with all the litter changed out weekly followed by a deep cleaning of the cage monthly.

Both mice and rats are clean in their habits and do best on pellet foods, which are simple to dispense. When you give your pets fresh treats (see the section on nutrition in

Chapter 4), uneaten portion will need to be removed to prevent spoilage and mold growth.

What do mice, rats, and dormice eat?

Mice and rats will eat just about anything, but that is not the nutritional approach you want to take. Chapter 4 discusses regulating the diet of these little animals to achieve the correct mix of protein, carbohydrates, vitamins, minerals, and fiber. This is best accomplished with pre-formulated pellet foods.

Dormice have a different diet because they are, by nature, tree dwellers. They will need more seeds and grain, as well as some nectar and live foods like crickets and mealworms. The live food is more labor intensive on your part, but not difficult to dispense.

Refer to Chapter 4 for more detailed lists of specific foods that are acceptable (and unacceptable) for each of these companion rodents.

How much water do pet rodents need?

Regardless of type, you should give your pet rodent a constant supply of clean, fresh water. The most efficient water bottles hang on the side of the habitat and dispense the liquid through a ball bearing tip. This method keeps debris from getting in the water and prevents the liquid from spilling into your pet's bedding.

What kind of cage should I get?

There is great debate about the best habitat for animals of this sort. Rats and mice do well in aquariums with a second story wire "topper," while dormice need a more vertical arrangement that will replicate their natural arboreal tendencies.

The real considerations are that your pets have enough room, that the temperature in the enclosure can be adequately regulated, and that they are safe from both escape and attack from other pets in the household.

To understand more about considerations of space, ventilation, and form factor, please see the relevant portions of Chapter 4. Please note that the chapter also discusses cage placement, which is a crucial consideration. No habitat should ever be placed in a draft, or in direct sunlight.

Chapter 8 – Breeder Directories

Rat Breeders – U.S.

California

Ratz Realm Rattery - http://www.ratzrealm.com
Breeding dumbo, rex, and hairless in blue, champagne and chocolate. Located in Pasadena

Bleu Royale Rattery - http://www.freewebs.com/bleuroyale
Sign the guestbook, have a look at the resident rats, and see available/future litter prospects. Located in Sacramento.

Blue Skies Rattery - http://blueskiesrattery.tripod.com
Small rattery located in Selma - Specializing in blues, minks, and blacks in dumbo and top-eared. Also rex and standard fur. Occasional litters available.

Fuzzy Misfits Rattery - http://www.angelfire.com/sd2/cindys_rattery/page3.html
Formerly known as Cindy's Rattery. Breeding dumbos, rexes and top eared rats in various colors and markings. Located in San Diego.

Colorado

Colorado Mountain Meadow's Rattery - http://www.coloradorattery.com
Adoptions, babies, odds and ends. Located in Aurora.

Florida

Bellaratta's Nest - http://bellaratta.homestead.com
Specializing in dumbo rats

Georgia

Phoenix Gate Rattery - http://www.pxrats.com
Breeding mink, Siamese, selfs, hairless, dumbo, rex,
miniatures and merles. Located in Statesboro.

Idaho

Curly Whiskers Rattery -
http://curlywhiskersrattery.tripod.com
Breeding hairless dumbo and standard, Siamese and Blue
in Dumbo, Standard and Rex. Located in Boise.

Illinois

Sweet Genes Rodentry - http://www.sweetgenes.com
Breeds for quality in type and sweet in temperament.
Located in Naperville.

The Dumbo Tree Rattery -
http://www.freewebs.com/dumbotree
Adoptions, sales, first-time rat owner advice, and letters
from people who have purchased/adopted from this
rattery.

Maine

Darling Road Rodentry -
http://darlingroadrodentry.tripod.com
See current litters, adoption policies, or see if you have a rat
this rattery would like to buy for their breeding program.

Michigan

Silver Fuzz Rattery - Breeding standard, dumbo and rex
rats with various colors and markings. Located in Dorr

Rat Dippity Rattery - http://www.ratdippityrattery.com
Specializing in healthy, friendly, pet rats that are wonderful
human companion animals, in various colors, coat types,
ear types and patterns/markings.

Ohio

River Rats Rattery - http://riverratsrattery.tripod.com
RMCA member, breeding rexes and dumbos in fawn, pearl,
blue. Located in NW Ohio

Raffin House Rattery - http://www.raffinhouse.com
Breeding for health and temperament, specializing in blues,
mink, agouti and black eyed white. Located in Fremont

Jenni's Mischief - http://www.jennismischief.com
Breeding a variety of colors and coat types. Includes
pedigree information and photographs. Located in
Brunswick

Pennsylvannia

Rattenburg Rattery - http://www.angelfire.com/psy/chic-k-rat Small rattery in central Pennsylvania focusing on breeding tame and healthy Siamese, Himalayan and other color varieties in rats.

Washington

Rattie Rascals Rattery - http://www.boardmanweb.com/rattery/rascalsrattery.htm Includes research for genetics and ownership has been placed on this rattery's homepage. Located in Port Orchard.

The Daisy Chain Rattery - http://users.palouse.com/rparsons/daisychain.html Breeding healthy happy rats. Located in Pullman

The Breakfast Bunch Rattery - http://breakfastbunchrats.weebly.com Breeding high quality Dwarf Rats, High Whites, Dumbos, and sometimes Hairless. Color and coats vary; pedigrees included. Located in Renton

West Virginia

Curiosity Rats - http://www.curiousv.com/curiosityrats Breeding for temperament and type, specializing in marked and Siamese standards. Located in West Virginia.

Rat Breeders - UK

Source: nfrs.org

South East England

Sarah and Dan Byrne (Evenflow Rattery)
Crawley, West Sussex RH10
Website: http://www.evenflow-rats.co.uk
Aiming to breed Berkshire and variegated in topaz, buff
and cinnamon with associated varieties.

Doug Connor (Tenebrae Stud)
Banbury, Oxon OX16
Telephone: 07989 666 864 Home: 01295 369205
Email: douglas.connor@gmail.com
Roan & striped roan. Silvered black & Chocolate and ivory.

Angela Corrie (Milliways Rattery)
Southampton, SO16
Website: http://milliwaysrattery.co.uk
Siamese, Russian blue point Siamese, black and Russian
blue.

Fiona Coull (Zappa Stud)
Eastleigh, Hampshire SO50
Website: www.zapparats.co.uk
Variegated, capped and Berkshire in
topaz, agouti and cinnamon in top ear only.
From Autumn 2012 -Burmese, Russian Burmese and black
in dumbo and top ear; possibility of other varieties.

Rhiannon Eustace (Little Rats Rattery)
Bishop's Waltham, Hampshire SO32
Telephone: 01489 896994 Mobile: 07988 065211
Website: http://littleratrattery.wordpress.com
Berkshire, British blue, Siamese in red and black eyes. All in
dumbo and top-eared.

Ellie Goddard (Shatterlings Rattery)
Hastings, East Sussex TN34
Email: violetellie@yahoo.co.uk
Russian blue and related varieties in top ear and dumbo.

Jazmine Huddy (Labyrinth Rattery)
Cranleigh, Surrey, GU6
Telephone: 07930 397085
Website: http://labyrinth-rattery.webs.com
Breeding for temperament in dumbo/top ear, smooth, rex
and double rex in a variety of colors.

Natasha Klus (Elkwood Stud)
Southsea, PO4
Website: www.elkwoodstud.webs.com
Breeding for platinum, platinum agouti, British blue and
related varieties.

Katy Lang (Faeriemead Rattery)
Chobham, Surrey, GU24
Telephone: 07735 252245
Website: http://faeriemeadrattery.deviantart.com
Aiming for first litters in January 2014:
silvered black and Siamese.

Kate Mitchell (Bibby's Rattery)
Hermitage, Berkshire RG18
Telephone: 07810 692852
Email: kate.j.mitchell@googlemail.com
Breeder of Cinnamon, cinnamon pearl and pearl, martens
and agouti. Sometimes rex and dumbo.

Rackie Powell (Symphony Stud)
Reading, Berkshire RG7
Telephone: 0118 9744 695 Mobile: 07961021159
Website: http://www.symphony-rats.co.uk
Ivory, black, some black eyed
Himalayan/golden Himalayan

Felicity Shields (Ramkin Rattery)
Banbury, Oxfordshire OX16
Telephone: 01295 272023 mobile: 07914 941198
Breeding Russian Burmese (dumbo and rex) and Martens -
at the moment those are occurring in normal, Russian and
silver agouti.

Veronica Simmons (Kropotkin Stud)
South East London SE12
Telephone: 020 8852 4008
E-mail – vjsimmons@btinternet.com
Pearl with mink, cinnamon and cinnamon
pearl. No dumbos.

Ann Storey (Rivendell Stud) &
Holly Storey-Smith (Topthorne Stud)
Dartford, Kent DA1
Mobile: 07770 800521
e-mail: ann@rivendellrats.com
Agouti, chocolate, lilac agouti, lilac, occasional Russian blue, chinchilla, argente cream, platinum agouti, squirrel, cinnamon, silver fawn, champagne, buff. No dumbos or rex.

Alison Triggs (Valiance Rattery)
SW London, TW12
Website: www.valiancerats.co.uk
Black, chocolate, mink, coffee, champagne, British blue and lilac (occasionally agouti versions and/or Irish markings).

Heather Ukwuajoku (Maidenhair Rattery)
Havant, Hampshire PO9
Websites: www.maidenhair-rattery.weebly.com
Agouti, Russian Blue with related colours.
Marked and self in different coat types.

Adrienne Vallender (Hibiscus Rattery)
Southampton, Hampshire SO16
Telephone: 02380 222275 or 07432 201562
Website: http://hibiscus-rattery.weebly.com
Breeding for temperament in black eyed Siamese (blue and seal point), British blue, Russian blue, Russian silver and possibly Martens.

Jayne Warren (Warrensark Rattery)
Southsea, Hampshire PO4
Telephone: 02392780420 mobile: 07793 864575
Working towards Russian topaz, but will get related
varieties along the way such as Russian blue, agouti and
topaz. Some rex.

Holly Wells (Sweet Rattery)
Chatham, Kent, ME4
Telephone: 07896 544419
Website: www.facebook.com/sweetrattery

Sharon Williams (Seagull Stud)
Brighton, East Sussex, BN41
Telephone: 01273 381154
Mobile: 07701 080529
Website: www.fuglyrats.co.uk
Double rex in top & dumbo. Rex & smooth top & dumbo.
Cinnamon Pearls, marked, Burmese and others.

Katie van Zyl (Callisto Stud)
Reading, Berkshire, RG2
Website: www.callistorats.co.uk
Variegated, Berkshire & Badger in Russian Blue & Dove,
often resulting in Cinnamon, Mink, Agouti and Black. Top
ear, smooth coats only.

South West England

Fiona Barker (Adelphe Stud)
Padstow, Cornwall PL28
Telephone: 01841 520168
e-mail: creeky@tiscali.co.uk
Chocolates, various pets

Natalie Burge (Midsomer Mischief Rattery)
Midsomer Norton, Somerset, BA3
Telephone: 07980 396150
Website: https://www.facebook.com/MidsomerMischief
Agouti, blue agouti, black, roan, hooded, Berkshire, top-eared & dumbo. New varieties in the future. We breed for health and great temperament.

Jackie Cairns (Jacaranda Rattery)
Stonehouse, Gloucs., GL10
Telephone: 07747 612869
Email: jackiescairns@yahoo.co.uk
Russian Blue, agouti, black in Essex and unmarked. Top ear and dumbo.

Julie Davis (Belyaev Rattery)
Longlevens, Gloucester, GL2
Telephone: 01452 540244 mobile: 07985 233723
Email: acrorats@gmail.com
Breeding blues, Siamese and mink along with other colours resulting from these matings.

Amy Foxford (Cupcake Rattery)
Bugle, near St. Austell, Cornwall PL26
Website: www.cupcakerats.co.uk
Breeding Buff, Chocolate, Black, Agouti and Topaz. In top ear, smooth and rex coat.

Jenna Murton (Hakuna Matata Stud)
Cheltenham, Gloucestershire GL51
Telephone: 07981 735160
Website: http://www.hkmrats.co.uk
BE/RE Seal/Russian Siamese, Black and Russian Blue, some dumbo and rex. Occasionally have others.

Julia Oldham (Hillway Rattery)
Somerton, Somerset TA11
Telephone: 07528 476981
Email via: https://www.facebook.com/HillwayFancyRats
Martens, Silver agouti, Russian blue, Russian silver, British blue. Occasional blue point satin Siamese. Mink. Black self and Berkshires. Working towards merle and hooded martens.

Sarah Stevens (Milo Stud)
Bristol, BS13
Mobile: 07787 860400
Website: www.milostud.co.uk
Downunders in hooded ,Spotted and patched, hooded & various marked rats, Topaz,Buff (no dumbo) , Siamese (ruby eyed no dumbo) in smooth , rex also
dumbo in marked rats

East of England

Nelly Brewer (Merriment Rats)
Kings Langley, Herts WD4
Website: http://www.merrimentrats.co.uk
Breeding for marten and related varieties, red eyed and black eyed, top ear and dumbo

Patricia Burn (Ouzle's Rattery)
Godmanchester, Cambs, PE29
Telephone: 01480 434311
Website: http://homepage.ntlworld.com/pataburn/patsrats
Russian, Burmese, B.E. Siamese, black and occasionally others incl. British/powder blue and striped roan.

Sarah Collier (Fantasy Rats)
Benfleet, Essex SS7
Telephone: 01268 756175 mobile 07757 696534
Email: sarah@pocoblu.com
Agouti, Black, Cinnamon, Mink; Occasional Siamese and Burmese. In self, Irish, and Berkshire with smooth and rex coats.

Jane Finbow (Mulberry Stud)
Glemsford, Suffolk, CO10
Telephone: 01787 282198
Email: afcredit@yahoo.co.uk
Website: http://www.mulberryrats.com
Chocolate, buff & champagne with smooth coats (hopefully coffee one day) and topaz & agouti in rex and smooth coats.

Mary Giles (Zephyr Stud)
Meldreth, Cambridgeshire SG8
tel. 07814 652594 - texts only after 7pm please
Website: http://www.zephyrrats.co.uk
American mink and cinnamon, some chocolate based.
Platinum, quicksilver and their agouti versions. Will also
have black and agouti

Lisa Grove (Halcyon Stud)
Lowestoft, Suffolk NR33
Telephone: 01502 501570
Website: http://halcyonrats.weebly.com
Agouti (smooth & rex); Topaz (smooth and
rex); Russian Blue, Russian Blue Agouti & Russian Topaz;
Black and Agouti Hooded (smooth and rex); Golden
Himalayan & Siamese. All the above are Top Ear (I do not
breed Dumbo)

Ian Hayward-Chamberlin (Mossbrook Rattery)
Great Cambourne, Cambridgeshire, CB23
Telephone: 07903 216909
Email: ianmhayward@hotmail.com
Hooded and variegated.

Anne Holmes (Ansbrook Rattery)
Rayleigh, Essex SS6
Telephone: 01268 778630
Website: http://www.ansbrook.co.uk
Burmese, Siamese, Essex, British blue, Cinnamon pearl,
topaz, Russian blue. Marked, rex, dumbo.

Tanya Rawlinson (Ionian Stud)
Watton At Stone, Hertfordshire. SG14
Telephone: 07912 250891/07554 354509
Website http://www.ionianstud.co.uk
Breeding for British Blue, Black, Cream & Related Varieties.
All Top Ear, I do not breed for Dumbo

Hannah Newman (Rainveil Rattery)
Colchester, Essex CO12
Email: glorfindel.goldenflower@gmail.com
Marked, roaned and self rats in various colours including
Russian Blue, Dove, Pearl, Champagne, Buff and Black. Top
eared and Dumbos

Julie Oliver (Valhalla Stud)
Wisbech, Cambridge PE13
Telephone: 01945 465663 mobile: 07971 919363
Email: julieanneoliver@msn.com
Pink eyed white, ivory, cream.
Pearl, sometimes in rex.
Occasional russian blue marked and dumbo pets.
Breeding towards cinnamon pearl essex

Joanna Pierre (Epiphany Stud) &
Danielle Panton-Pierre (Twilight Dreams Rattery)
Westcliff on sea, Essex SS0
Email: epiphany_jo@hotmail.com
Epiphany - Agouti, cinnamon, topaz, silver
Fawn, British blue, British Blue Agouti, Non-Marked and
Essex. Occasional Russian blue dumbo Twilight Dreams –
Dumbo

Jem Quarry (Figwit Rattery)
Bedford, Bedfordshire MK41
Telephone 07807 842093
Capped/masked and shaded

Sheila Sowter (Flaxholme Stud)
Brentwood, Essex CM15
Telephone: 01277 221839
Email: sas24@btopenworld.com
Breeding for genetic information. Marked rats. Rex,
Siamese, Pet quality dumbos, others from time to time.

Midlands

Lloyd Allington (Eximius Rattery)
Lincoln LN1 1PZ
Telephone: 07809 864597
Website: www.eximiusrats.webs.com
Agouti, black, American mink & American cinnamon in
both dumbo & top ear.

Lynn & Mike Bailey (Serenity Rattery)
Bilston, Wolverhampton WV14
Telephone: 0121 530 1514
Website: http://serenityrats.webs.com
Black, British blue, British blue agouti, agouti.

Arianne Callicott & Elizabeth Seal (Pumpkin Rattery)
Central Leicester LE3
Telephone: 07895 544887
Website: www.pumpkinrattery.weebly.com

Black and mink masked, capped and variegated with satin and standard coats in dumbo. Burmese and Russian Burmese. Russian blue agouti in rex and standard in dumbo. Cinnamon in rex and standard. Chocolate. Marten. Any related colours/varieties.

Sarah Chamley (Sunshine Rattery)
Grimsby, N.E. Lincolnshire DN37
Telephone: 07792 475310
Website: http://sunshinerats.weebly.com
Russian blue, Russian blue agouti, black, Siamese and Russian blue point Siamese (black and red eyed) top eared and dumbo. Smooth coat only

Gemma Corfield (Gemstone Rattery)
Willenhall, West Midlands WV12
Telephone: 07941 841007
Website: http://www.gemstone.vze.com
Russian Topaz and Russian Blue Agouti in rex. Possibility of dumbo.

Lisa Cross (Clarke) (Swiftvalley Stud)
Rugby, Warwickshire. CV21
Telephone: 07866 516 299
lisajclarke16@gmail.com
Mink self Capped in Cinnamon British Blue Agouti

Daniel Fearn (Origin Rattery)
Rednal, Birmingham B45
Telephone: 07725 083248
Website: http://originrats.weebly.com
Martens, Russian Burmese and related

varieties, all in top eared and dumbo.

Coleen Gruber (Skatta Rattery)
Grimsby, Lincolnshire DN34
Website: http://skattarat.co.uk
I aim to breed good tempered, healthy rats for pet homes
and possibly showing. I breed top eared and dumbo in both
smooth and rex coats. Breeding black, champagne, silver-
fawn, agouti, chocolate & related colours/varieties.

Lucy Hunt (Destiny Stud)
Welford, Northants, NN6 6HR
Website: http://destinyrats.weebly.com
Russian silver, will get related colours like Russian blue
and British blue.

Debbie Lauf (Beltane Rats)
Dudley, West Midlands
Website: http://beltanerats.webs.com
Berkshire and Irish in Russian blue, Russian blue agouti,
black and agouti

Rebecca Hinson (Mercury Stud)
Great Barr, Birmingham B43
Telephone: 07519084880
Black, Russian blue, Russian blue agouti, Russian blue
point Siamese and dumbo Lynda Lazarevic (Brammocks
Rattery) Raunds, Northamptonshire NN9
Telephone: 01933 622 076 Mobile: 07876 684 954
Website: http://www.brammocksrattery.co.uk
We breed for Russian blue varieties, Burmese and Siamese

Vicki Meakin (Campion Stud)
Syston, Leicestershire LE7
Telephone: 07790 371153
Website: http://campionstud.weebly.com
Russian blue and Russian blue agouti in top ear and
dumbo. Berkshire, badger and hooded in mink and
cinnamon - top ear only.

Kyra Murray & Tom Bunce (Atlas Rattery)
Loughborough, Leicestershire LE11
Telephone: 01509 265541 mobile: 07540 846609
Russian blue/Russian blue Essex, Russian blue
agouti/Russian dove agouti, and related varieties in top
eared and some dumbo

Lian O'Sullivan (Rowangate Stud)
Corby, Northamptonshire NN18
Mobile: 07725035471
Website: http://www.rowangate.co.uk
Variegated & striped roan. Russian blue.
Rb agouti. Agouti & black.

Annette Rand (Brandywine Stud)
Rugby, Warwickshire CV22
Telephone: 01788 817763
Email: rattycorner@internettie.co.uk
Website: http://www.rattycorner.com
Russian blue and Russian blue agouti in Essex and
unmarked. Other colours sometimes available

Eleanor Cadman (Yabba Dabba Doo Stud)
Swinfen, Staffordshire WS14
Mobile: 07729459980
Email: e.k.thurley@gmail.com
Website: http://www.freewebs.com/yabbadabbadoorattery/
Buff, topaz, agouti, pearl, cinnamon pearl, cinnamon and
pink eyed whites. dumbos and rexes in some of the
varieties

North of England

Emma Bond (Stardust Rattery)
Scawthorpe, Doncaster, DN5
Website: http://stardust-rattery.weebly.com/
Breeding for Burmese, Wheaten Burmese, Siamese and
Russian varieties in top ear and dumbo.

Julie Botterill (Muddiwarx Rattery)
Glossop, Derbyshire, SK13
Telephone: 07966 394 692
Email: Juliebot@aol.com
Breeding for hooded, roan and hooded downunder in black
and mink, top eared and dumbo, smooth and rex coated.

Christine Bowen (Rats4life Rattery)
Whinmoor, Leeds LS14
Telephone: 01138 083287
Website: http://www.rats4life.zoomshare.com/
RE & BE Siamese, Russian blue, Russian pearl, Cinnamon
pearl, Planning Russian blue agouti and Russian blue point
Siamese, golden Himalayan in the future.

Stacey Cochrane (Honeyduke Rattery)
Fulwood, Preston PR2
Telephone: 07745 547368
Email: HoneydukeRats@gmail.com
Website: http://honeydukerats.weebly.com/
Breeding for silver agouti and black eyed silver agouti, also black and agouti.

Jemma Fettes (Isamu Rattery)
Ashton-on-Ribble, Preston PR2
Telephone: 07563 603130
Website: www.isamu.weebly.com
Black and agouti in top eared and dumbo with the chance of American mink and related varieties

Shelley Harris (Aeris Rattery)
Wallasey, Merseyside CH44
Telephone: 07792 720706
Website: http://www.freewebs.com/aeris-rats/
Russian blue, russian dove, topaz and agouti, other varieties sometimes available

Kayleigh Hartley (Outlaw Rattery)
Wilberfoss, Yorkshire YO41
Telephone: 07411 002942
Email: kayleigh_h66@hotmail.com
Breeding for Champagne, Chocolate and Pink eyed Whites in top ear and dumbo. In both smooth coat and rex.

Kelly Heys (Sundrop Rattery)
Lancaster, Lancashire LA1
Telephone: 07956 423802

Website: www.sundroprats.co.uk
Currently breeding agouti and black in Essex and unmarked with silver fawn and champagne in the future.

Laura Holt (Stovokor Rattery)
Appley Bridge, Wigan WN6
Telephone: 07535 510559
Website: http://stovokorrats.weebly.com/index.html
Breeding for Russian Blue, Blue Agouti & Russian Dove Agouti in smooth, Rex & Lustrous coats. Golden Siamese & Burmese in smooth/Recessive Rex coats, chance of Velvet. Top ear & Dumbo.

Lilly Hoyland (Lilliput Stud)
Walkley, Sheffield S6
Website: http://www.lilliputrattery.co.uk/
Breeding for Russian Blue Dumbo, Quicksilver and Spotted/Hooded Downunder

Beri Instone (Amarandh Rattery)
Thirsk, North Yorkshire YO7
Telephone: 01845 527369
Website: http://www.amarandh-rats.co.uk/
Breeding for American-based havana. Will also expect black, agouti, American mink, American cinnamon, chocolate, chocolate agouti, chocolate American cinnamon. Smooth coats in dumbo and top eared.

Catherine Mace (Gallifrey Rattery)
Morley, West Yorks. LS27
Email: contact@gallifreyrattery.com
Website: www.gallifreyrattery.com

Roan and striped roan in black and agouti:
top ear and dumbo. Also likely to get self, hooded and
Berkshire and silver fawn. Working on Russian silver and
Russian silver agouti in autumn 2014.

Lisa Maurin (Lovecraft Rats)
Lancaster, Lancashire LA1
Telephone: 07792 948976
Website: http://www.lovecraftrats.co.uk/
Black, agouti, cinnamon and mink. Essex and unmarked.

Nick Mays (Trinovantum Stud)
31 Theobald Avenue, Doncaster,
South Yorkshire DN4 5AY.
Website: http://www.donnyrats.webs.com/
Silver Fawn, Champagne and Ivory.
Himalayan in rex and smooth coats (both eye colours).
Working on Golden Himalayan.

Lizzi McIntee (Ratoon Stud)
Middlesborough, Cleveland
Telephone: 077980110996
Website: http://ratoonrattery.piczo.com/
Breeding for essex (occasional dumbos), russian siamese
(red eyed and black eyed) and topaz/agouti

Kate and Kevin Rattray (Rattray Stud)
Rodley, Leeds LS13
Telephone: 01132292531 or 07811004361
Website: http://www.freewebs.com/rattrayrattery/
Breeding for Russian blue self and
Berkshire in various ear/coat type

combinations. Also breeding for martens
Anita Richardson (Omega Rattery)
Aintree, Liverpool, L9
Telephone: 07779 385290
Email: omegarats@hotmail.co.uk
Striped Roan, Roans and Russian pearl.

Janette Rogers (Stillyrats Stud)
Stockton, Cleveland TS21
Telephone: 01740 630285
Website: http://www.freewebs.com/stillyrats/
Russian Blue, Russian Blue Agouti, Agouti,
Siamese, Burmese, Ivory , Pearl/Cinnamon Pearl, Essex in
Top eared and Dumbo Smooth Coat and Rex

Ceredwen Slattery (Sunset Rattery)
Kearsley, Bolton, Lancs. BL4
Telephone: 01204 704646
Blue, white and other colours of dumbo rat.

Sheena Stratton (Bog Myrtle Stud)
31 Theobald Avenue, Doncaster,
South Yorkshire DN4 5AY.
Website http://www.donnyrats.webs.com
Variegated, Hooded, Berkshire and Badger; Argente
Creme, Silver Fawn, PEW and Champagne all in rex and
smooth coats. Working on Apricot Agouti.

Jannine Taylor (Endeavour Stud)
Telephone: 07933 647386
Rothwell, Leeds, LS26
Website: http://www.endeavourrats.webs.com/

Siamese, Burmese, Russian blue and Russian blue agouti.

Laura Viarisio (Methyl Rattery)
Withington, Manchester M20
Telephone: 07581 207590
Website: www.methylrattery.weebly.com
Breeding for stable health and temperament in agouti roan and topaz, dumbo and top ear, standard coat and rex coats, with plans to make Russian topaz in the future. Agoutis, blacks and buffs expected as a result of test matings and improving rex coats. Plans to make coffee based doves, and related varieties in dumbo and top ear, with standard and rex coats in the near future.

Scotland

Emma Buckley & Bas Brouwer (Tailbearer Rattery)
Neilston, Glasgow, G78 3HX
Telephone: 07877 535674
Email: crushed-rose@hotmail.com
Not started breeding yet. Aiming for good temperament and hoping to breed badgers/blacks.

Toyah Leitch (Hawthorn Stud)
Cambuslang, Glasgow, G72 6WF
Telephone: 07828 772 981
Email: enquiries@hawthorn.org.uk
Website: www.hawthorn.org.uk
Silver fawn, agouti. Black, champagne, chocolate. Russian blue and Russian dove.

Marten, silver agouti. Hooded, downunder hooded.
Karen McDonald (Breagha Rattery)
Cowdenbeath, Fife, KY4 9JE
Telephone: 01383 514395 mobile: 07518 517136
Email: breagharats@sky.com
Website: www.breagharats.webs.com
Variegated, agouti, cinnamon

Anna McKinnon (Ralston Stud)
Ralston, Paisley, PA1 3AL
Telephone: 07811 970206
Website: www.ralstonrats.co.uk
Topaz, agouti, rex.

Rhona Robertson (Scunnerbug Rattery)
Balloch, West Dumbartonshire, G83
Website: https://www.facebook.com/ScunnerbugRats
Breeding for happy healthy pets in Berkshire and
variegated - sometimes in rex and dumbo.

Ireland

Laura Jones & Karl Woods (Bongo Fury Rattery)
Ballinascarthy, Clonakilty, Cork
00353 238869142
Website: http://www.irishrats.co.uk
(regularly travel to Leeds and South Wales so can deliver to
both) - Breeding for Russian varieties in standard coated
top ears, and Cinnamon Pearl and related varieties in rex
and standard coated top ears
Mainland Europe
Magdalena Karczewska (z Wuwuniarna Rattery)

Bialobrzeska 9/35

02-379 Warsaw

Poland

Telephone: +48 518 957 758

Email: wuwunka@aim.com

Breeding for all pedigree and health. Varieties are less important to me. I am interested in bases: Mink, Topaz, Russian Blue,, Martens without points and markings: recessive badger & blazed other varieties. Top ears, sometimes dumbo & smooth hair

Romana Kastlova (Gremleen Rattery)

Nechvilova 1844, 148 00 Prague, Czech Republic

Telephone: +420 608 529 518

Email: romanakastlova@seznam.cz

Website: www.chk-gremleens.estranky.cz

British blue line – top and dumbo ears, smooth, rex and wav coat. Siamese line – top and dumbo ears, smooth and rex coat. Harley line – top and dumbo ears, smooth, wavy, harley and harley satin. Russian blue, black and Siamese colour.

Katerina Ungrova (X-Rats Rattery) Kartouzska 6, 150 00 Prague, Czech Republic

Telephone: +420 605 356 945

Email: katka.ungrova@gmail.com

Website: http://www.chsx-rats.estranky.cz/

British blue line: top and dumbo ears, smooth and rex coat. Siamese line: both black and ruby eyes including golden himilayan with top and dumbo ears, smooth and rex coat.

Elise W (Rattery Castor)
Venlo, The Netherlands
Email: contact@ratterycastor.nl
Website: www.ratterycastor.nl
Breeding for Russian blue (agouti) and Russian silver (agouti), hooded and Berkshire markings, smooth coated and top eared.

Mouse Breeders – U.S.

Connecticut

The House of Mouse
www.freewebs.com/thehouseofmouse

Indiana

What The Cat Dragged In
www.whatcat.wordpress.com

Kansas

Little Loves Mousery
www.facebook.com/pages/Little-Loves-Mousery/444716415539380

Kentuckey

Jack's Mousery
www.jacksmousery.com

Maryland

Mason Dixon Rodentry
www.masondixonrodents.com

Michigan

Silver Fuzz Rattery
www.silverfuzzrattery.com

New Hampshire

Storybook Pocket Pets
www.freewebs.com/storybookspocketpets/index.htm

New Jersey

Darby Mousery
www.darbymousery.wordpress.com

Ohio
Mousykins
www.mousykins.info

Oregon

Runaway Mousery
www.runawaymousery.weebly.com

Pennsylvania

CS Beck Rodentry
www.csbeck.com

Texas

Martingale Mousery
www.freewebs.com/martingalemousery

Washington

Twitching Whiskers Mousery
www.twitchingwhiskersmousery.com

Mouse Breeders – UK

Faluma Mousery
http://mousery.faluma.us

Jingles Mousery
www.sites.google.com/site/jinglesmousery
Wolf Magic Rattery
www.freewebs.com/wolfmagicrattery

Bumblebee Mice Mousery
www.bumblebeemice.synthasite.com

Painted Skys Mousery
www.paintedskiesmousery.webs.com

Dormice Breeders

Finding dormice of any type for sale is a hit or miss proposition. Many mouseries and ratteries do breed dormice, but they do not necessarily advertise the fact.

I recommend that you begin with www.fancymicebreeders.com to look for sources in the United States, and www.preloved.co.uk for dormice for sale in the United Kingdom.

In almost any discussion forum where fancy rodent enthusiasts gather, you will see the occasional reference to dormice for sale, but they are quite difficult to find. Expect to search for a source for some time before locating these creatures.

Afterword

I began this book with two stories about rodents that led me to become fascinated with these little creatures who, even as wild animals, live on the periphery of our world.

The tiny field mouse that found its way into the bathroom where it had a run in with my mother came into our house looking for the "good stuff" humans have to offer, whether that was food or bedding material.

The cotton rat my classmates and I accidentally captured has long lived in my mind as one of the greatest examples of an instinctive, native intelligence at work.

I now know that rats are indeed the smartest of all the rodents, and that domesticated rats easily learn tricks and assimilate language well beyond their own names.

As for dormice, I have only second-hand knowledge of these tiny and bright beings, but like all rodents they have a whimsical way about them with their over-sized eyes and charming personalities.

Their growing popularity as "pocket pets" earned them a place in this book, but I would regard dormice as a "specialty" rodent, suitable for advanced enthusiasts only.

In our crowded and busy world, companion rodents have a lot to offer us as pets. They are clean, have minimum husbandry needs, and are intelligent and interactive.

Afterword

If you want a companion animal, but have neither the space nor the time to devote to a dog or cat, a rat, mouse, or dormouse could be the perfect option for you.

As I said in the beginning, I hope you will at least come away from this book with a greater appreciation for these animals and free of the stereotypical perception that rodents are filthy, diseased vermin.

They are, in fact, quite clean and pose no zoonotic disease threat to the humans with whom they live. And as for this business of a "rat" being a sneaky or somehow underhanded fellow, you'd be hard pressed to find a more affectionate pet.

If you do decide to bring a rat, mouse, or dormouse into your life, you are the one who will be caught in the trap of fascination these little spirits so cleverly set. They are, in a word, irresistible!

Relevant Websites

American Fancy Rat and Mouse Association
www.afrma.org

The History of Fancy Mice
www.afrma.org/historymse.htm

Rat and Mouse Club of America
www.rmca.org

Fancy Mouse Breeders' Association
mousebreeders.org

Fancy Mice Breeders Forum
www.fancymicebreeders.com

East Cost Mouse Association
www.eastcoastmice.org

The National Mouse Club
www.thenationalmouseclub.co.uk

The London & Southern Counties
Mouse and Rat Club
www.miceandrats.com

South Eastern Mouse Club
semouse.webstarts.com

The Scottish Mouse Club
thescottishmouseclub.webs.com

Relevant Websites

Australian National Rodent Association
anraq.tripod.com

Australian Rodent Fanciers' Society of NSW, Inc.
ausrfsnsw.com

Australian Rodent Fanciers' Society Qld. Inc.
www.ausrfsqld.com

Russian Mouse Fanciers
www.miceland.ru

The Finnish Show and Pet Mice Club
www.hiiret.fi

Netherlands Mouse Club
www.kleineknaagdieren.nl

Polish Mouse Club
www.pmcorg.webd.pl

Deutsche Mause
(German Fancy Mouse and Mongolian Gerbil Association)
www.dmrm.de

SVEMUS (Swedish Mouse Club)
www.svemus.org

Glossary

A

agouti - A coloration in which each hair is marked by alternating bands of color.

albino - Characterized by a complete absence of pigment in the skin and coat.

B

bedding - The substrate used in the base of a companion rodent's cage, for example, ground corn husks, wood shavings, or shredded newspaper.

C

crepuscular - Animals exhibiting their greatest level of activity at dawn and dusk.

D

dormice - Rodents found in Europe, Africa, and Asia. Members of the family *Gliridae*. They are roughly 2.4 to 7.5 inches (6-19 cm) and weigh 0.53 to 6.35 ounces (15-180 grams).

dumbo rat - Rats with large, round ears placed to the side of their heads.

F

fancy mice / rats - Domesticated mice and rats bred to specific standards that are suited to life as companion animals and often for competition in judged shows.

feeder mice - Mice raised in bulk to be sold as live feed for snakes, large lizards, and other similar pets.

G

gestation - The duration of a pregnancy from conception to birth.

gremlin - A gremlin mouse with one normally placed ear and one positioned on the side of the head.

H

herbivore - Animals that consume plants as their daily source of nutrition.

hypoallergenic - Any substance or animal that is not likely to cause an allergic reaction in sensitive individuals. Companion rodents are not hypoallergenic.

L

laboratory rats/mice - Rodents bred to be kept in laboratories and used in medical and scientific research. One of the earliest uses of these animals was the development of genetic theory by Gregor Mendel.

litter - This term can either refer to multiple offspring born to one parent, or as an alternate reference to substrate or bedding (the material used to line small animal habitats.)

M

mouse - A small mammal in the family *Rodentia* that has small rounded ears, a pointed snout, and a hairless tail.

N

nest box - A small box (cardboard, wooden, or ceramic) in which a companion rodent sleeps, hides, and plays.

nesting material - Soft material, either fiber or shredded paper, given to companion rodents to line their burrows and/or sleeping areas.

nocturnal - Nocturnal animals sleep during the day and are most active at night.

P

phenols - Oils present in aromatic shaved bedding like pine and cedar that can cause respiratory problems and liver damage in many small animals.

R

rats - Rodents that are similar to, but larger than mice, with pointed snouts, and long, sparsely haired tails. All true rats are members of the genus *Rattus*.

rex - Mice and rats that exhibit crimped or curled whiskers and fur that lies in waves.

rodent - Gnawing mammal in the order *Rodentia,* which is the largest of all the mammalian orders. Examples are rats, mice, dormice, squirrels, hamsters, porcupines, and similar creatures.

rosette - Mice with whorled fur on each hip that spirals in opposition to the main coat.

S

self - Fancy rats and mice whose body is all one color.

substrate - An alternate term for material lining the bottom of a small animals habitat. Also known as bedding or litter.

T

tan - A fancy mouse or rat with a solid colored upper body and a golden tan belly.

W

wild rats / mice - Undomesticated rats and mice that have not been cultivated in planned breeding programs to live as pets. Although they can, in theory, be caught and tamed, they never really settle down comfortably to life with humans.

Index

Milton Keynes UK
Ingram Content Group UK Ltd.
UKHW021837070923
428247UK00009B/558